'BLUE-COLLAR BALLIN'

The Playbook for Industrial Athletes

BY:

ANTHONY R BARBER JR

Dedicated to my son's

"Sebastian & Amari"

TABLE OF CONTENTS

INTRODUCTION

BLUE COLLAR BALLIN' – THE PLAYBOOK FOR INDUSTRIAL ATHLETES

Welcome to Blue Collar Ballin': The Playbook for Industrial Athletes.

This is not just another self-help book; it is a roadmap for mastering your life as a blue-collar professional in a rapidly evolving world. Whether you are in the manufacturing sector, skilled trades, or STEM fields, or a side hustle monster the rules for success have changed, and it is time to play the game smarter, not just harder. In the pages that follow, we will dive deep into the strategies and mindsets that can transform your career and personal life. You will discover how to Master the Clock and make every second count with time management techniques that maximize productivity. We will explore the importance of Iron Body, Steel Mind, where we will break down fitness routines designed for longevity, ensuring you are not just surviving but thriving in physically demanding environments. The power of a Growth Mindset is often underestimated, but here, you will learn how adopting an infinite game approach can keep you ahead of the curve, continuously adapting and learning. In today's interconnected world, it is not just what you know, but who you know. That is why we will also cover Network or Never, a chapter dedicated to leveraging connections that can propel your career forward. Knowing when to stick it out and when to move on is a crucial skill, covered in Knowing When to Pivot. We will discuss how to recognize signs that it is time for a change and how to do it strategically. As you progress, you will see how important Certifications are in giving you an edge over the competition—proving that sometimes, a piece of paper can unlock doors to new opportunities. For those in or considering the STEM fields, STEM-Ing Ahead will guide you through the complexities and vast potential of science and technology careers. If you are in the skilled trades, Mastering the Craft will help you navigate your path to expertise, ensuring that your hands-on skills are in high demand. We will also walk you through the intricacies of the manufacturing sector in Navigating the Factory Floor—because understanding the environment you work in is half the battle. Efficiency is not just a buzzword; it is a way of life that can drastically impact your success, as you will learn in Efficiency is Key. Setting realistic goals is vital to your journey, which is why Goals that Grind is dedicated to helping you establish and achieve ambitions that are both practical and impactful. Finally, we will explore how a Self-Improvement Mindset can keep you on a path of continuous growth, and how Managing Your Environment can create spaces that support your success, both physically and mentally. Each chapter is designed to be a playbook, offering you actionable insights and tools that you can apply immediately. The goal? To equip you with a Roadmap and strategies needed to not only survive but thrive in your field. Because in the game of life, industrial athletes do not just work—they ball. Let us get started.

I have always prided myself on my ability to observe, analyze, and breakdown a situation, a person, or my environment, which in many ways led me to ask questions. One of those questions being "why does the skilled individual get labeled as a simple "Utility" by society as well as the work environment, but the lifestyle very rarely reflects the output, and time invested by said individuals? The separation, and pseudo workplace classification politics has done a number on the mindset of many, especially that of Men in my view. The thought of working a so called, "dirty job" is a major turn-off within this modern era to many when you compare it to the soft-life view of an office environment surrounded by female counterparts and the smell of chai lattes. That might be an exaggeration in a few instances, but I will proudly stand by my statement, nevertheless. Humans have grown flabby and soft when it comes to the Mind, which seems like a weird thing to say when you consider all the technological advancements of the last 20 years. I would argue that for all the benefits afforded by technology…it allows for a gradual erosion of the human, mind, body, and soul, if left unchecked. In this information Age, we have been conditioned to not only accept the negative critiques and rebukes of others as 100% valid, but our natural default has been reduced to people pleasing and admiration seeking. The allure of social media highlights has brainwashed many into a mental bottleneck without them realizing the trap until it is too late in many cases. The powerful tool of social media has become a poison pill in western society as it creates pseudo competition between people, with zero incentive to compare yourself with a ghost. As I stated in my previous book: "Build or Destroy: The guide to grinding…" your only opponent is the self."

Many today have grown dependent on "smart phones" to tell us everything, we cannot exercise without music playing in our ears, and when it comes to consistent, productive, and rewarding work, we view it as boring activity. We rather, hit the easy button and flee the scene at the first sign of a single bead of sweat. Entitlement sits at an all-time high in western society, due to our addiction to "Convenience." Convenience is the silent thief of ambition. When you become addicted to the easy route, you start sacrificing the very things that build character and strength. Every time you choose convenience over effort, you are chipping away at your potential. It is like taking the short path on every journey; sure, you get there faster, but you miss the experiences that teach you resilience, patience, and grit. There is no substitute for challenging work, only the tradeoff of laziness and a perpetual downward spiral. Convenience creates a false sense of achievement—you are busy, but not productive. You are moving, but not progressing. Real growth happens in discomfort, in the struggle. That is where you learn to push past your limits, to innovate, to build something real. When you rely too heavily on convenience, you are not just weakening your work ethic; you are also weakening your mind. You stop thinking critically, stop solving problems, and start depending on shortcuts. In the end, those shortcuts will shortchange your success. So, if you want to build, if you want to truly grow, you must reject the allure of convenience. Embrace the hard road less travelled because that is where the true rewards lie.

PLAYBOOK #1

"TIME IS MONEY: "MASTERING THE CLOCK"

We all heard the phrase, "Time is Money" but I would like to translate the phrase for the people in the back of the room.

Time is Money when the human energy flow is guided and efficient. When you think of the 9 to 5 workplace, the one feature of that environment that typically stands out is the "Timeclock". You know, that ridged device usually mounted on a wall Adjacent to an entry or exit reminding us how much of an inconsistent P.O.S we are when we are late. Just like this typical "Timeclock" ...the timeclock of life does not discriminate, its simply documents your consistency or lack thereof. There are consequences for being late, as it shows your dedication to being inconsistent. The clock is simply a gauge for your behavior on a base level, to keep you on the correct path, and to keep you accountable. If you show up early, late, or exit the workplace early it is all documented. I will tell you a secret you might not be aware of; "Life keeps an open ledger every second of every day" ...many just ignore this fact. I personally experienced both the benefits and drawbacks of poor time management. I was recruited early in my Aviation career by a very prominent fortune 500 military contractor. The opportunity came with many benefits that could be leveraged, one of those being free tuition assistance. Just for your information for anyone not living in the west, most notably (the United States) college is one of the costliest actions a person can and will make. I reframed from referring to college as an investment because most never properly leverage their education to generate a significant (ROI) return on investment.

In my case I failed to take full advantage of this free opportunity from the onset, meaning I failed to get focused and put my nose to the grindstone from day one of my hire date. Now many can and will read that and say…" but you went to school eventually, so what's the big deal!?" The big deal came in the form of time wasted…time wasted being cocky that I acquired a great paying job in my early/mid 20's, time wasted in the form of partying on the weekends (wasted time & money) with people that I do not even communicate with currently 10 years later. The overall wisdom I gained by not moving with a sense of urgency from the onset was the time clash. The single, unmarried, childless version of myself that should have started school in 2011 and finishing by 2013 directly clashed with the older, married, father version of myself that choose to go back 2018. While I managed to finish in impressive fashion if I do say so myself, time never faltered or cared for any of the extra responsibilities I choose to add to my life. Yes, it forced me to be creative, innovative, and compromising which are all stronger traits I now possess…fact remains, I had to bow down to father times harsh discipline. I missed precious time with my son, because I had to study late or spend a whole weekend drafting a research paper.

Something that should have been an overall easy breeze activity slowly turned into a chore, a labor, or job due to poor initial time management on my part. Hindsight is of course 20/20, but it is my duty to inform you especially about the power and leverage of youth.

Please understand that you will be older longer than you will ever be younger, this too belongs to the riddle of time. I since then move with a sense of urgency as much as possible to maximize my prime year energy, and it has become a Boone for myself as well as my beneficiaries. Time and money are intricately linked, and understanding their relationship is crucial if you want to truly excel. Simply put, time is money. Every second, minute, hour you waste is potential income lost. In the grinding world, where every moment counts, you need to realize that every second you squander is a missed opportunity to build wealth, health, improve your skillset, or advance your career. But let us break it down even further. Money is not just currency; it is a representation of energy—specifically, the energy you put into your work. When you exchange your time for money, you are converting your energy into a tangible asset. If you are inefficient with your time, you are wasting your energy. If you mismanage your time, you end up working harder for less return. Think of it this way: when you waste time, you are depleting your energy reserves without a corresponding gain in financial or personal growth. The more effectively you manage your time, the more efficiently you channel your energy, and the greater your financial rewards. It is a direct correlation—effective time management amplifies your energy output, which in turn maximizes your earning potential. Consider the example of any high-achiever—whether it is an entrepreneur or a top-level executive. They understand that time is their greatest asset. They do not waste it on trivial matters. They allocate their time strategically, which allows them to focus their energy on activities that yield the highest returns.

This focused energy translates into financial success because they are not just working hard; they are working smart. In the grind, it is not just about putting in the hours; it is about making those hours count. The better you manage your time, the more efficiently you convert your energy into financial gains. So, if you want to build, if you want to truly succeed, you need to respect the value of your time. It is the key to unlocking your full potential and turning your energy into tangible results.

"A ruler that failed to measure"

Time is the one thing that even the most successful people in history could not afford to waste. Look at someone like Napoleon Bonaparte. Here was a man who rose to power rapidly, building an empire that stretched across Europe. His military genius was undeniable, and his strategic mind unmatched. But in the end, it was not just his enemies that brought him down—it was his mismanagement of time. Napoleon's invasion of Russia in 1812 is a prime example. His decision to invade was driven by ambition, but his failure to properly account for the time it would take to achieve victory proved disastrous. He underestimated the Russian winter and overestimated how quickly he could conquer such a vast land. As time dragged on, his troops were worn down not by battle, but by the harsh elements and lack of supplies. By the time he realized his mistake, it was too late—his army, once mighty, was reduced to a fraction of its size, and his empire began to crumble. Napoleon's downfall was not just a result of poor strategy—it was a failure to respect the clock. He thought he had more time than he did, and it cost him everything. This is the lesson you need to learn: Even the most powerful can be brought down by the mismanagement of time. You can have all the talent, resources, and ambition in the world, but if you do not respect time, you are setting yourself up for failure. Do not let your grind be derailed by the same mistake. Recognize the value of every minute and treat it like the asset it is. Time waits for no one, and neither should you.

"Mastering Spacetime"

Time management is not just a concept; it is the engine that drives success. Look at Elon Musk, a prime example of what happens when you master your time. Musk, the CEO of SpaceX, Tesla, and several other ventures, is notorious for his obsessive focus on managing every minute of his day. He is not just busy; he is strategically maximizing every second. Musk uses a technique called 'time blocking.' He schedules his entire day into five-minute slots. That is right—five-minute increments. This method keeps him on track and eliminates wasted time. He does not let a single minute slip away without purpose. For instance, his day is meticulously divided into blocks for specific tasks, meetings, or deep work sessions. This intense focus ensures that he is not just moving; he is making real, measurable progress. He also practices task batching—grouping similar tasks together to cut down on the time wasted switching between various kinds of work. By handling all meetings or project reviews in one block, he stays in the zone and keeps his productivity high. This approach is not about efficiency; it is about maintaining peak performance throughout the day. Musk also applies the '80/20 rule'—focusing on the 20% of tasks that generate 80% of the results. This prioritization helps him cut through the noise and zero in on what really drives progress. It is this strategic focus that has enabled him to revolutionize industries and lead multiple groundbreaking companies. Musk's success is not about working hard; it is about working smart. He set the bar high by turning time management into a powerful tool for achieving extraordinary goals.

You want to build something great, take a lesson from Musk. Structure your days, prioritize relentlessly, and make every moment count. That is how you turn your grind into massive success and make a real impact. Time is a resource you cannot afford to waste, not even in the small pockets of your day. Yes, even those brief moments you might spend on the toilet can be leveraged for productivity. It is all about using every second wisely and turning idle time into opportunities for growth. Your smartphone, when used correctly, can be a powerful tool in this endeavor.

Here a few ways you can make the most of your time, and that portable computer you call a smartphone, even in those unexpected pockets:

1. **Educational Podcasts and Audiobooks:** Use those moments to listen to podcasts or audiobooks that expand your knowledge. Whether it is industry trends, motivational content, or personal development, these resources can keep you learning and growing without needing extra time in your schedule.

2. **Skill Development Apps and websites:** There are numerous apps/websites designed for skill-building and learning. Whether it is language apps, coding challenges, stock trading/investing, basic skills such as cooking or brain-training exercises, you can work on improving your skills in short bursts.

3. **Review and Plan:** Use this time to review your to-do list or plan your day. Many productivity apps allow you to quickly jot down tasks, set reminders, or review your goals. It's a fantastic way to stay organized and ensure you are on top of your responsibilities.

4. **Networking and Communication:** Respond to emails, messages, or networking opportunities. Quick, focused responses can help maintain connections and keep projects moving forward, even in brief intervals.

5. **Mindfulness and Reflection:** Use this time for brief mindfulness exercises or reflection. Apps offering guided

meditation or reflective journaling can help you stay centered and focused, which can be beneficial for overall productivity.

6. **Micro-Learning Modules:** Engage with micro-learning platforms that offer short, focused lessons. These are perfect for quick learning sessions and can fit into even the briefest of breaks…yep even when you're sitting on that porcelain throne.

The key is to recognize that every moment can be an opportunity if you approach it with purpose. By integrating productive habits into these small windows of time, you're not only making the most of your day but also reinforcing a mindset of continuous improvement. Remember, the grind isn't just about the big pushes; it's about consistently using every available moment to push closer to your goals, in small but effective increments. Even on the toilet during your incremental escapes from reality, you can be building, learning, and growing. Make every second count.

Only currency that truly matters at the end of the day (Time). You can lose money and earn it back, but time? Once it's gone, it's gone for good. Many individuals know this fact to be true, that every second wasted is a piece of your life you can never reclaim. That's why mastering the clock is the first step in mastering your life. In this world, there are two types of people: those who let time slip through their fingers and those who grip it tightly, making every moment count. If you're serious about grinding—about building something real—then you must treat time like the precious resource, it is. You must harness it, monitor it, and make it work for you. That means slowly limiting excuses (until you have little to none), and elimination of procrastination. It's about discipline—choosing to do what needs to be done even when you don't feel like it. Time management isn't just about organizing your day; it's about taking control of your future. You need to understand that every minute you spend, you're either investing in your success or giving it away to distractions. The clock is always ticking, and LIFE doesn't wait for anyone. So, ask yourself: Are you going to let time pass you by, or are you going to master it and turn it into the foundation of your success? The choice is yours, and the time is now, so let's get to it my friend.

PLAYBOOK #2

"IRON BODY, STEEL MIND: FITNESS FOR LIFE"

You cannot teach work ethic you smart, dumb motherfuckers…you have it, or you do not! Those words still permanently burned into my subconscious by one of my favorite teachers, let us call him "Mr. C." Mr. C was one of my instructors during my time in aviation school. He was an old-school, hard-ass, zero nonsense type of instructor. He would always say: "I promise to tell you the truth and give you everything you need to succeed…but you have to put in the work". Pretty straight forward way of teaching you could say, but you would be surprised at how many faltered in his classes. Not due to some debilitating mental condition, or speech impediment, nope, it all came down to a lack of confidence and focus. Mr. C taught basic and advanced electrical, as well as mechanical and electrical theory. Youd be surprised how many people dropped out after a few weeks of instruction. Every legit Aviation school is overseen by the (FAA) federal Aviation Administration, which holds each school, and instructors to strict standards, which in-turn holds each student to ridged standards as well. We had to adhere to strict time constraints, for example, each minute you attended class was tracked in real time by the instructor. If a student was late by 1 minute, you were logged in as 6 mins late. In aviation, every minute an aircraft is grounded it is burning through money, and if were talking military aircraft, every minute the warfighter sits grounded means its less time to save lives. Referring to the previous chapter, this is another example of how critical time management is in all aspects. Whenever a student dropped out or simply started dragging ass, as he called it.

Mr. C emphasized the importance of mental fatigue without training and proper mindset implementation. Not only was he held to account when it came to attendance, but you in turn had to make up every single minute of missed time before you received full credit for that block of instruction. He'd (Mr. C) would go on to say…you're only as good as your habits. He'd expound by saying; "if you sleep late, you'll rise late, if you eat dinner late, your body will waste energy on digestion instead of repairing damage and recuperation". Longevity is not about getting lucky, he'd say; it comes down to good habits and preemptive measures. He was retired Army, so he had an ingrained disciplined frame, but one couldn't help but listen and take his words as a gift. At the time, He was in his mid-50's and yet his physical fitness trumped many of us in the class even if we were athletes or gym rats…his aura literally reflected his discipline.

He (Mr. C) ran 5km every day and did calisthenics (body weight exercises) to remain fit, which is a simple routine, but the results were apparent. I started to implement his philosophy into my own life also, and I must say, it is one of the best decisions I have made as it afforded me a body that is always optimum, and a mind that remains focused on the task at hand. I have even ran a half marathon (15.6 mi) trail race due to my consistent training routine. Additionally, I do not require caffeine, or stimulants to "wake-up" or stay alert throughout the day like many. I subscribe to a monthly meal prep service also, which grants me flexibility, portion-controlled food, and additional time to work on getting better, along with things that genuinely interest me. Thanks Mr. C for going hard and never letting your foot off the gas.

Survival of the fittest has never been more of a potent phrase, especially in this new information age. Not because the playing field is increasingly violent, but because it's extremely easy to thrive now, which consequently makes it easy to remain lazy as well. That statement might go over the heads of many readings this but allow me to explain; Understand this…you have zero competition, absolutely nobody walking the planet compares to you, in fact, you are a "one of one" walking around. Confidence often shows its face after enough incremental victories, meaning you must show & prove to "yourself" first and foremost. The mind needs evidence so the heart (your will) can power your motives and gauge moves properly. Most young western males for example are living inward, meaning their more reclusive, less focused on fitness, easily rattled by life or the words of others, with social media contributing to this mental decline. The moment you log into your social media account, you find yourself swept up into a storm of comparison, i.e., "The highlight reel". Social media is a double-edged sword. On one hand, it connects us, gives us a platform to display what makes us truly unique, and allows us to showcase our grind. On the other hand, if you're not careful, it can drag you down, especially as a man navigating today's world. Let's get real about how social media can contribute to male depression— something that's backed up by research and data. Here's the deal: social media isn't just a highlight reel; it's a distorted version of reality. You're bombarded daily with images and posts from other people—guys showing off their successes, their chiseled bodies, their luxury lifestyles. It's easy to get caught up in that and start comparing yourself, thinking you're falling short because you don't have what they have. But what you're seeing is just surface, a curated version of someone else's life, an elaborate movie montage. When you start measuring your worth against that, it can mess with your head. According to studies, heavy social media use is linked to increased rates of depression and anxiety, especially among men. One reason is the constant comparison to others, which can lead to feelings of inadequacy and low self-esteem. You see what seems like everyone else winning, and it can make you feel like you're failing. But here's the thing—most of what you see online is filtered, edited, and polished to perfection. You're comparing your behind-the-scenes with someone else's highlight reels, and that's a losing game at the highest level. Another aspect of social media that contributes to depression is the lack of real, meaningful connections. It might seem like you're connected to hundreds or thousands of people, but how many of those connections are authentic?

The superficial interactions online often replace real-life relationships, leaving you feeling isolated and lonely, even when you're constantly 'connected. Data shows that this loneliness can be a significant factor in depression, particularly for men who are already less likely to seek help or talk about their struggles. Let's not forget about the pressure to always be 'on.' Social media creates this expectation that you've always got to be grinding, awake, pushing, always hustling, and always achieving. News flash my guy; all three takes time, attention, and massive amounts of energy. That constant pressure can lead to burnout, stress, and ultimately, depression. When you're constantly trying to live up to an unrealistic standard, it takes a toll on your mental health.

How do you protect yourself?

You've got to recognize that social media is a tool, not the truth. Use it to your advantage, but don't let it dictate your self-worth or your happiness. Be aware of the traps—comparison, isolation, and pressure—and take steps to disconnect when you need to. Focus on building real connections, set boundaries for your social media use, and remember that your value isn't determined by likes, followers, or any other metric online. Your true grind is about what you're doing in real life, not what it looks like on a filtered screen. Understanding how social media can contribute to depression, you can take control and use it as a tool for growth, networking, and business expansion not as something that holds you back. Keep your mind strong, stay focused on your real-life goals, and don't let the illusions of social media cloud your vision."

One brick at a time should be mantra of every person striving to improve themselves. Reading books, overall healthy diet & mental health routine, consistent exercise, meditation, building meaningful relationships, with powerful networking groups all serving as foundational building blocks for the future. The bricks are a complete waste if the mortar (the mind) can't hold it all together at the end of the day. You have a vehicle, it eventually needs maintenance, correct? So why are you waking up every day for years on end trying to convince yourself that your own body, mind, doesn't need regular maintenance and upkeep. You fail to wash the dirt and insects from you Windshield, guess what, your delusional ass won't be able to see the road ahead. Humans often look like what we put ourselves through. Iron Body, Steel Mind—this isn't just a catchy phrase; it's the core of what it takes to not only survive and thrive in the industrial world, but in real life. If you're serious about longevity, you've got to build a body that can take the hits and a mind that can push through any inevitable obstacle. This isn't just about getting by; as I said, it's about longevity—staying strong, sharp, and ready for whatever comes your way, no matter how tough the job gets. In the industrial fields especially, your body is your most valuable tool. It's what carries you through long shifts, handling heavy workloads, and handling the steady grind day in and day out.

But here's the thing: if you're not treating your body like a well-oiled machine, it is, you're setting yourself up for breakdowns. In this game, breakdowns don't just cost you a day's work—they can cost you your future.

You might be shocked to hear that industrial athletes receive similar or more intense injuries that some professional sports athletes. Here's the part of the game you might not know…that job, or corporation won't fit the bill for a full body rehab and recovery like our professional sports athlete counterparts have access to. Tear your ACL/MCL, suffer a spine or shoulder injury and you will see even with so-called "good health insurance" that you will be put through your paces as you must fight or often jump through hoops to get the correct treatment you need to fully recover. At the end of the day, it comes down to money and resources.

Something that does not get enough attention during daily life—how a major health injury can wreck your life, not just physically, but financially. In America today, the sad truth is that most people are one severe injury away from financial ruin. And if you are out here grinding in the industrial fields, in skilled trades, or STEM jobs, the risks are real. A slip, a fall, a subtle moment's mistake, and suddenly you are looking at weeks, months, even years of recovery. Here is the kicker— most Americans simply cannot afford to take that kind of hit. According to recent data, 40% of U.S. households would struggle to cover a $400 emergency expense. Now, imagine if that emergency was not just $400 but thousands of dollars in medical bills, lost wages, and ongoing treatment. It is no wonder that medical expenses are the leading cause of bankruptcy in the United States. For the average household, a major health injury does not just strain finances—it can completely derail them. Let us say you are the primary breadwinner, pulling in a steady paycheck that keeps the lights on, the rent paid, and food on the table. If you are suddenly unable to work because of an injury, the ripple effects are immediate and devastating. Savings get drained, bills start piling up, and the stress of trying to make ends meet adds up fast. We are not just talking about physical pain anymore—we are talking about the mental and emotional toll that comes with financial stress, which can lead to anxiety, depression, domestic issues within the household, and even more health problems. This is not just theory; it is reality for millions of Americans every day. Without proper health insurance, without a financial safety net, and without a plan to cover the unexpected, a major injury can set you back years. Even with insurance, the out-of-pocket costs can still be overwhelming. Deductibles, co-pays, and the lost income from being out of work can quickly turn your financial situation upside down. That is why it is crucial to take your health seriously—not just to avoid injury, but to protect your future. Investing in your physical fitness is not about looking good; it is about building a body that can handle the demands of your job, everyday life, and reduce the risk of injury. It is about making sure you are strong, agile, and durable, so you can stay in the game and keep earning. Also, remain mindful about being smart with your money. You must build that emergency fund, secure the right insurance, and think ahead, because the truth is, grinding hard is not about today—it is about being ready for whatever comes tomorrow, dig me!

Do not wait until an injury puts you on the sidelines to start planning. Prepare now, so that if the worst happens, you are ready to handle it without losing everything you have worked so hard for. Remember, part of being an industrial athlete is being proactive—not just in your work, but in your life. Protect your body, protect your mind, and protect your financial future by being proactive and utilizing a bit of foresight. That is how you stay in the game, no matter what life throws your way. Do you want to be the broke and broken old man…or the bossed-up & Ballin old man!?…be mindful and move with intention.

Common Injuries in STEM, Skilled Trades, and Manufacturing Fields

- **Cuts and Lacerations** - Often caused by sharp tools, machinery, or materials.

- **Fractures and Broken Bones** - Resulting from falls, being struck by objects, or accidents involving heavy machinery.

- **Muscle Strains and Sprains** - Frequently due to heavy lifting, repetitive motion, or awkward postures.

- **Back Injuries** - Caused by improper lifting techniques, repetitive strain, or prolonged standing.

- **Eye Injuries** - From exposure to chemicals, flying debris, or improper use of safety glasses.

- **Burns** - Resulting from contact with hot surfaces, chemicals, or electrical sources.

- **Hearing Loss** - Due to prolonged exposure to elevated levels of noise in industrial environments.

- **Chemical Burns and Inhalation** - From improper handling or exposure to hazardous chemicals.

- **Crush Injuries** - Caused by being caught between or under heavy machinery or objects.

- **Amputations** - Often a result of machinery accidents, particularly in manufacturing environments.

- **Electrocution** - Occurs in environments where workers are exposed to live electrical circuits.

- **Repetitive Strain Injuries (RSIs)** - Caused by repeated motions, leading to conditions like carpal tunnel syndrome. Respiratory Issues - From inhaling dust, fumes, or other airborne particles in manufacturing environments.

- **Slips, Trips, and Falls** - A common cause of injuries across all sectors, often leading to fractures, sprains, or head injuries.

- **Head Injuries** - From falls, being struck by objects, or machinery-related accidents.

- **Heat Stress and Heatstroke** - Particularly in hot manufacturing environments or outdoor skilled trades.

- **Joint Injuries** - Often due to repetitive motion or strain from heavy lifting.

- **Foot Injuries** - From dropping heavy objects or stepping on sharp items.

- **Crush Injuries** - From getting body parts caught in machines or between heavy objects.

- **Lacerations from Tools** - Cuts caused by improper use or malfunctioning of tools and equipment.

General Injury Trends

STEM Fields: While traditionally less physically hazardous, there are risks associated with laboratory work, such as chemical burns, eye injuries, and repetitive strain injuries.

Skilled Trades: Injuries often stem from manual labor, tool usage, and exposure to the elements. Strains, fractures, and cuts are common.

Manufacturing: Heavy machinery and repetitive tasks lead to a higher incidence of crush injuries, amputations, and repetitive strain injuries.

Building an iron body is not about looking good; it is about being resilient. You need strength, endurance, and mobility—not just to get the job done today, but to keep doing it for years to come. That means putting in the work now, in the gym, on the track, and in your kitchen. It means understanding that every rep, every run, every meal is an investment in your longevity. But it is not just about the body. You can be as strong, but if your mind is not right, you are still going to fold under pressure. A steel mind is what separates those who thrive from those who just survive. It is about mental toughness, focus, and the ability to push through when everyone else is ready to quit. The grind is as much a mental game as it is physical, and if you are not training your mind to handle the stress, the setbacks, and the challenges, you are leaving yourself exposed. So, if you want to stay in this game for the long haul, you must build both—an iron body and a steel mind. That is your foundation for longevity. That is how you stay in the game, keep winning, and push forward no matter what life throws at you. This is your blueprint—now it is time to get to work.

Here's a hard truth that a lot (especially men) overlook:

Your body is not always going to operate at peak performance. As you age, things change—especially when it comes to testosterone, the hormone that fuels your strength, energy, and drive. Research shows that male testosterone levels start to decline as early as age 30, and it is not a slow drop, either. On average, testosterone decreases by about 1%

each year after 30. That might not sound like much at first, but by the time you are in your 40s and 50s, that decline can add up to a significant loss in muscle mass, energy levels, and overall physical performance. This drop in testosterone is not about your body—it is about your mind, too. Lower testosterone levels can lead to reduced motivation, lower confidence, and a decline in cognitive function. That means if you are not taking advantage of your youth—when your testosterone levels are at their highest—you are missing prime years to build your empire, make your mark, and push yourself to new heights in your career.

Now, don't get it twisted—this does not mean you are not destined for sudden decline as you age, but it does mean that the energy, strength, and resilience you have in your younger years are invaluable assets that you should be leveraging to the fullest. When you are young, you can put in those extra-long hours, take on those physical challenges, and recover faster. You can push harder and go further than you will be able to later. In your youth, you have the chance to build a strong physical foundation and set the stage for long-term success. This is the time to grind efficiently, to put in the work, and to take risks in your business and or career. It is when you should be laying the groundwork for the future, so that when you do hit those later years, you are not just coasting—you are capitalizing on the powerful base you have built. Consider the greats in any field—athletes, entrepreneurs, leaders—they did not wait until their 40s or 50s to start making moves. They took advantage of their youth, used their high energy levels, and pushed their limits when their bodies were most capable. This is your time to do the same. Do not let these prime years slip by while you are on the sidelines. Get in the game now, build that iron body, sharpen that steel mind, and set yourself up to dominate both now and in the years to come. The grind does not stop, but the way you grind will change as you age. Use your youth to establish yourself, to create momentum that carries you forward, and to build something that lasts. Because when your body starts to slow down, you will be glad you pushed hard when you had the strength to do so. Sometimes the counterintuitive way of thought is that part of the minds journey we should attack the hardest…self-made truly taste better.

"Conditioned for Greatness"

Let us talk about historical examples of the benefits of having an "iron body, steel mind," and how it can be the edge that puts you ahead of the competition. Think about Muhammad Ali, the greatest boxer to ever step into the ring, and not just because the brother had hands. Ali was not just a master of strategy or mental toughness—his physical foundation was unmatched in his prime era. He trained his body to be a finely tuned machine, and that is what allowed him to outpace, outlast, and outfight any opponent who dared to challenge him. Ali was never the biggest or the strongest heavyweight, but he was the most conditioned. His legendary training regimen included everything from roadwork in the early hours of the morning to countless rounds in the ring, honing his skills and sharpening his endurance. He built his body into a beautiful weapon—a tool that could go the distance in the toughest fights. This training became most apparent when he faced George Foreman in the famous 'Rumble in the Jungle,' most people thought he did not stand a chance against the younger, stronger Foreman. But Ali knew that while strength fades, conditioning and strategy endure. Ali used his physical foundation to wear down Foreman, letting him punch himself out while conserving his own energy for the perfect opportunity to present itself. This was a gamble by many accounts, but his body was ready for punishment. When the moment was right, Ali struck, proving that a strong body, combined with a sharp mind, could outlast, and outsmart any competition. It was not about how hard he could hit; it was about how long he could keep going, how much punishment he could take, and how effectively he could leverage his strength to achieve victory.

This lesson:

During the grind, you are going to face competition—whether it's on the job site, in your career, or in life. While everyone else might be looking for shortcuts or relying solely on talent, you will have the upper hand if you have built a strong, resilient body & mind that can endure the pressure and keep pushing forward when others start to fade, and trust (they will). Your physical foundation if cultivated properly over time is what will give you that fine razor edge, creating smooth penetrations and transitions. It is what will allow you to work longer, recover faster, and handle the toughest challenges without breaking down. It is what separates those who burn out from those who keep grinding, year after year, achieving greater and greater levels of success. Building that iron body, strong mind is Essential for the long haul, after all this is a marathon, not a sprint. Make it strong, make it resilient, and use it to outpace anyone who tries to stand in your way. With a body & Mind like that, you are not just competing—you are dominating.

PLAYBOOK #3

"THE INFINITE GAME: CULTIVATING A GROWTH MINDSET"

We live in an era of abundant information, and this useful sword often cuts both ways because of the over confidence that develops because of being a pseudo know-it-all. Many never feel the need to retain information, since it is so readily available, while others struggle to implement a single thing in real time because of the multitude of choices and or strategies available. Seems like paralysis by analysis is too commonplace today, with the majority stuck in an idea cycle which unfortunately, compounds indecision. I too at one time suffered with this very thing, and I must admit, even now it can be a struggle to make decisions especially when you want so desperately to hit a home run on the first swing. I had to ignore the high batting average mentality for a second and keep my focus on the bottom-line..." the basics." As we go through this playbook, you will soon notice how everything relates to everything else. Growth for example takes time, which we have discussed the importance of, along with the importance of discipline as it relates to health in the iron body/steel mind playbook chapter. Growth is often painful as it brings us back to a sense of zero, starting line, base level or however you prefer to phrase it. The point is, we humans are in a constant state of flux as we struggle against our inherited bubbles of confinement, i.e., societal norms, religious dogma, past self-weakness, insecurities along with generational curses. I have had the privilege of being able to break many generational curses handed down by my father and mother. I am a flawed human born to a set of flawed humans, so suffice to say, it was left up to me to write many wrongs and toxic mental leanings of my parents' generation. Allow me to tell you the backstory of China and Big-T. They both subscribed like many from their era to the "good enough" mantra. This seems like the quitter's school of thought when compared to a growth mindset mentality because it gives you an easy out effect button. Big-T's easy button came in the form of mismanagement of emotional energy due to his pre-mature divorce from his beloved China. Instead of doubling down on his natural skills in sales which allowed him to attract enormous amounts of income, he decided to fall victim to China's manipulative actions during the split. He decided to quit jobs to avoid child support obligations. Now those obligations were very extreme considering how much China has had it out for him, not to mention how bias the family court is when it comes to the mother. I say all of that to say, Big-T is highly intelligent, and more than capable of learning new skills, but he simply reserved himself to the mantra of "good enough" because of emotional stress and an unwillingness to get over the situation at hand.

So, he effectively stayed on the same level for the rest of his life due to a perceived boogey-man. He later would go on to tell me about his side during a conversation, and while I am naturally empathetic to his plight, I had to utilize his "Good enough" life choices as effective examples of what not to do, while traversing my own path.

China on the other hand choose to victim blame her way through life and leveraged her upbringings to double down on her "good enough" mentality. To be honest, she despises growth, because with growth comes with a hardline in the sand called accountability, discipline, and fearlessness of success... meaning everything is your fault. She went to nursing school and made it all the way to the end, studied hard for her final, but when test day came around, she failed by 2 points. Cavate to this is she had the chance to retest, not to mention her mother and her mother-in-law offered to babysit her child for her to effectively study for her retest. Sad to say, she effectively chose to go dance on a local television show ironically called "The place". In the end she used the excuse of being a single mother as the reason for not studying for the nursing retest. She would refuse to finish school and negate any chances for her to become a nurse. She used her school credits to fall into the nursing assistant tier of the medical realm. When asked and later confronted by her family members as to why she settled for a lesser position, she we on to say: "good enough". She would go on to work in the lower tier of medical services such as volunteering at elderly nursing homes or being a secondary care provider. While these positions are needed in society, the point here is that China choose a lower tier existence to escape the growth cycle that comes with elevating your station in life.

Let me tell you something about the 'good enough' mentality—it is poison to your potential. The moment you start thinking something is 'good enough,' you have already set yourself up for failure. 'Good enough' is the enemy of growth. It is that whisper in your ear telling you to stop, to coast, to settle. But here is the thing—if you are settling, you are not growing, and if you are not growing, you are falling behind. The growth mindset is all about pushing beyond what you think you can do and mastering that counterintuitive muscle. It is about seeing every challenge as an opportunity, every failure as a lesson, and every success as a steppingstone to the next level. But the 'good enough' mentality? It shuts all that down. It is like putting a cap on your potential and saying, 'This is as far as I'm willing to go.' You become comfortable, complacent, and satisfied with just getting by. Let me put it this way: having a 'good enough' mentality is like deciding to stop climbing a mountain because you have reached a beautiful view. Sure, the view might be good, but what about the peak? What about the heights you have not even seen yet? When you settle for 'good enough,' you miss the growth that comes from pushing yourself further, from going beyond your comfort zone, and from striving for excellence instead of just adequacy. In the grind, 'good enough' will not cut it. It is the mindset of those who are content with mediocrity, who do not want to put in extra effort, who do not want to take risks. But if you are serious about unlocking your potential, about reaching new heights, then 'good enough' can never be part of your vocabulary.

You have got to adopt a growth mindset—a mentality that says, 'I can always do more, be more, and achieve more. 'At the end of the day, 'good enough' is just a comfortable lie we tell ourselves to avoid the challenging work.' It is the straightforward way out. You are not here to take the effortless way out—you are here to grind, to grow, and to become the best version of yourself. That means never settling, never stopping, and never accepting 'good enough' as the final word.

Here is the thing about animals—they are hardwired for growth and success. You look at any creature out there, from the lion roaming the plains of africa to the bird in the sky, and you will see the same thing: instinct. Animals are born with a built-in blueprint for survival and success. They do not have to think about it; they just do it. The lion knows it needs to hunt to eat. The bird knows it needs to build a nest to stay safe. There is no hesitation, no second guessing—just action. They are in tune with their environment, always adapting, always growing, and always pushing toward success. But humans? We have something different going on. We are not just hardwired for survival; we have unlimited potential. And while that sounds like a blessing, it can also be a curse. See, animals do not have the luxury of choice—they do what they need to do because their survival depends on it. But we, as humans, can choose. We can choose to grind, to grow, to learn—or we can choose to be complacent, to settle, to stagnate. That is where the struggle comes in. With unlimited potential comes unlimited options, and not all of them lead to success. Unlike animals, we are not bound by instinct alone. We have minds that can dream, create, and imagine possibilities beyond our immediate survival. But with that power comes the danger of distraction, of getting comfortable, of taking the easy road instead of the grind. It is like this: imagine you are standing at a crossroads. One path is the grind—challenging, uncertain, and full of obstacles. The other path is comfort—easy, predictable, and safe. Animals do not get to choose; they are built to take the hard path because that is what keeps them alive. But you, as a human, you have the choice, and too often, that choice leads people to take the easy road, to settle for less, to stop pushing, to stop growing.

Harsh truth:

Your potential is a double-edged sword. It can take you to heights you never thought possible, or it can leave you stuck, spinning your wheels, never reaching your full potential. The difference lies in your mindset—in your willingness to embrace the grind, to adapt, and to keep growing, even when it is tough. So, what is it going to be? Are you going to tap into that unlimited potential and push yourself to grow like the lion, the bird, and every other creature that is hardwired for success? Or are you going to let that potential slip through your fingers, distracted by comfort and convenience? Remember, the animals in the wild are always on the move, always adapting, always growing because they do not have a choice. But you do. And that choice is what separates those who build from those who destroy. So, harness that potential, grind with purpose, and keep pushing yourself to new levels of growth and success. That's how you turn your potential into power."

The snail's pace.

"Let me drop a story on you about the humble snail. Yeah, I am talking about that little creature you never give a second thought to. Slow, steady, always on the grind, moving inch by inch, day after day. Now, most people see a snail and think, 'That's one slow, useless creature.' But there is more to that snail than meets the eye—just like there is more to you. See, the snail knows it is slow, but it does not let that stop it. Instead, it adapts. The snail does not sprint to its destination because it knows that is not its strength. Instead, it uses its environment, its sticky trail, to climb walls, cross rough terrain, and reach places others might think are impossible.

The snail does not complain about being slow—it just keeps moving, learning from every inch of ground it covers, and adapting to whatever comes its way. Now, imagine if the snail had the mindset of 'I'm too slow, so why bother?' It would never go anywhere. But the snail has a different mentality—a growth mindset. It understands that progress is progress, no matter how small. It does not get discouraged by its pace; it leverages its unique abilities, adapts to challenges, and keeps moving forward. That is what a growth mindset is all about— continuous learning, adaptability, and never stopping, no matter how tough the journey gets. In your grind, you must embrace that same mindset. You might not always be the fastest, the strongest, or the smartest in the room, but that does not mean you cannot outwork and outlearn the competition. It is about recognizing your potential, adapting to your environment, and continuously pushing forward. Every setback is an opportunity to learn, every challenge is a chance to grow, and every obstacle is a test of your resilience.

Just like the snail, you might not see massive leaps every day, but if you are moving forward, you are making progress. The key is to stay focused on the long game—learning, adapting, and grinding every single day. Over time, that slow, steady grind will take you further than you ever imagined. So, when life throws a challenge your way, remember the snail. Do not get caught up in how fast you are moving; focus on that. Keep learning, keep adapting, and keep grinding. That is how you unlock your true potential and turn each current step into future greatness.

Let me put you on game—if you want to increase your growth mindset in this modern era, you've got to approach it like you're training for the fight of your life. We are living in a time where information moves at lightning speed, and if you're not keeping up, you are getting left behind. So how do you make sure you're always in the game, always leveling up? Here is how. First, you've got to make learning your lifestyle. Not just something you do when you must, but a daily commitment. We're in the age where knowledge is everywhere—online courses, YouTube, podcasts, you name it. But here is the thing: you've got to be hungry for it. You cannot just coast on what you know now because the game's always changing. Make it a habit to soak up new skills, stay ahead of trends, and feed your mind with fresh ideas. You want to be the best? Then you've got to be the smartest "you" in the room, and that starts with never letting your mind go idle. Next, you've got to build a circle that challenges you. I am talking about surrounding yourself with people who will not let you get comfortable. In today's world, you have got access to connect with anyone, anywhere. Use that to your advantage. Find mentors who have already walked the path you're on, connect with peers who are hustling just as hard, and be around those who push you to be better every single day. The old saying goes, 'You're the average of the five people you spend the most time with.' So, if your circle isn't pushing you to grow, it is holding you back. Change that asap.

Now, let us talk about time. In this era, time management is not important—it is everything, just we covered in play book #1 You've got 24 hours, same as everyone else (well known fact by now), but how you use them makes all the difference. Leverage technology to stay on top of your grind. Use productivity apps, set goals with deadlines, and keep track of your progress. Make sure every minute is working for you. Whether it is setting aside time for deep work or squeezing in some learning while you're on the go, like when you're scrolling on your phone, you've got to be intentional with your time. You cannot afford to let a single moment slip away if you're serious about growth. And here is the kicker—do not be scared to fail. In this fast-paced world, if you're not failing, you are playing it too safe. Failure is not the end; it is just data. It is telling you what did not work so you can adjust and come back stronger. Look at all the big players out here—every one of them has faced setbacks, but they did not let that stop them. They learned, adapted, and kept pushing. That is the mindset you need to have. Every time you fall, you get back up smarter, stronger, and more determined. So, here it is: if you want to elevate your growth mindset, you've got to stay hungry for knowledge, surround yourself with the right people, manage your time like a pro, and never fear failure. This modern world is full of opportunities, but you've got to go after them with everything you've got. That is how you build, and that is how you destroy anything that stands in your way.

PLAYBOOK #4

"NETWORK OR NEVER: LEVERAGING CONNECTIONS FOR SUCCESS"

Where are you from, my guy? That was the first thing Joe hit me with the day we met. Joe—a hard-nosed, no-nonsense Hispanic man a few years older than me—asked this as he drilled a few holes into the aircraft structure we were working on. I was 26, fresh into a big aviation gig down in Texas, and Joe was already a fixture in the place. Family person, hustler at heart, always had something going on. But what got under my skin at first was Joe's habit of dipping out of the workflow to take phone calls. We would be deep in the grind, and suddenly Joe's phone would buzz, and he would be out, handling business while the rest of us kept pushing. One day, during a break, I straight-up asked him, "What's up with the non-stop phone calls, my brother?" Joe did not flinch—did not even get defensive. He just looked at me and said, "I'm handling business, Tone." That is when he let me in on it—he was in the middle of negotiating a property deal. Hustling on the side, even while he was grinding at the plant. I pressed him a bit, asked him about R.H., our supervisor. How was he getting away with stepping out so often? Joe just smiled and told me how he had built a solid rapport with R.H. long before I showed up. R.H. knew Joe could crank it up when it counted. We were in aerospace manufacturing, a high-stress, high-paced environment, and we were 75,000 hours (about 8 and a half years) behind schedule on the nacelle structure of the V22 tiltrotor aircraft. But Joe? He had the kind of relationship with R.H. that let him handle his side hustle without missing a beat. Here is the thing—I was so focused on the job that I overlooked the importance of building those connections. The team was new, the pressure was intense, and all I could see was the mountain of work in front of us. But Joe? He was playing a different game. He was building bridges with the OGs—R.H., Danny-boy, and K-dub, the guys who had been on that crew since they were 17, straight out of high school. These were the ones who knew the ins and outs, and Joe had their respect.

Where I came from, you always had to watch your back, double-check everyone's intentions. Trust was earned slowly, if at all. But Joe? He was a straight shooter from the jump. He would tell me like it was, even if he knew it would piss me off. "Tone, you're like my brother," he would say. "I see you more than I see my own family, so we might as well keep it real. "That was a turning point for me. I realized Joe and I were cut from the same cloth—we both had that drive, that hunger for something more. That connection became the foundation for something bigger. As the months rolled on, that bond spread throughout the crew. We all recognized one simple truth—we liked to get money, and we were better off doing it together. By the end of the year, we had an unspoken agreement—a brotherhood. No contracts, no formal deals, just a mutual understanding that we were going to help each other win.

Joe opened my eyes to the power of networking, not just in the boardroom but on the shop floor, in the trenches where we sweat and bled for a paycheck. Individually, we had our own strengths, but together, we were unstoppable. We turned our crew into a citadel of knowledge, experience, and opportunity. That is the game, right there. It is not just about what you do with your hands, but how you leverage your connections and mind. Whether you are negotiating deals on your lunch break or building bonds that will carry you to the next level, the relationships you build are your most powerful asset. In the grind of life, you do not make it to the top alone—you do it by locking arms with those who share your vision and drive. Another friend I met on this journey taught me the beauty of risk taking, his name was Dorian, often referred to as "The Spaniard". Dorian was from San Antonio and like myself was recruited by the same Aviation company a few months prior to my arrival on the scene. His main background strength was engines, or powerplant technology to be technical, still... My friend possessed a wealth of industry knowledge, not to mention he was well travelled and immensely cultured. After work when I still enjoyed an occasional drink, id join Dorian at the sports bar for a few after our shift, to talk business ideas and investment ideas. We shared a mutual respect, because as I mentioned before many of the individuals on my team valued the leverage potential money brought. Dorial acquired taste much like myself, meaning his demeanor and or philosophy did not always go over well with others, but it is this unique different life view that mirrored my own extreme views on diverse topics. He was one of the reasons I took my stock trading and investing mindset to another level. Before I met Dorian, I played around with options trading and took a few swing trades on a whim, but nothing too serious. The year was 2012, and everyone began returning from Christmas break and new year's. I remember that morning like it was yesterday, as Dorian walked up to me with that shit eating grin on his face with his arm extended. He said, "Senor, how the hell are you doing!?", to which I replied kindly; outstanding as usual my friend.

Dorian followed up swiftly saying; senor, are you ready for the green rush!? Of course, I did not understand what my spastic friend was referring to on any level. Weed senor, weed! Dorian blurted out, pumping his fist into the air as he chanted. Naturally, I said, what are you talking about now Dorian, and what does this have to do with me!? My friend promptly reminded me of the new bill that was slated to be signed into law in Colorado.

For context, when Colorado passed Amendment 64 back in 2012, it was not just a meaningful change for the state—it was the spark that set the whole cannabis industry on fire. Before this, marijuana was mostly an underground operation, with a few states having limited medical use. But when Colorado made recreational use legal, it shifted the conversation from backrooms to boardrooms, from the streets to the stock exchange. This was the moment the cannabis industry stepped out of the shadows and into the spotlight. The Colorado bill did not just legalize a substance; it legitimized a business, paving the way for a new wave of entrepreneurs, investors, and innovators who saw green—not just in the leaves but in the money to be made. Suddenly, there was a "Green Rush," with everyone from seasoned Wall Street investors to small-time stockholders wanting a piece of the action. On the stock market, companies tied to cannabis exploded, and Dorian and I took full advantage of this market shift, all via sharing information.

Everyone was looking to cash in on this new gold mine. Stocks of companies involved in the production, distribution, and even ancillary services like lighting and hydroponics systems saw their values skyrocket overnight. It was a feeding frenzy, with new cannabis companies popping up left and right, each one promising to be the next important thing. But here is the catch—just like any gold rush, there were winners and losers.

The market saw a lot of volatility because while there was enormous potential, there was also huge risk. The companies that thrived were the ones that had a solid business model, real growth potential, and the ability to navigate the complex legal landscape. Those who jumped in without doing their homework found themselves burned out and bankrupt. The Colorado bill was a defining moment, showing how quickly a shift in public policy could create an entire industry overnight. It was proof that when laws change, so does the market. But as with anything during this grind, success did not come to those who were just chasing a quick buck, or FastTrack advancement. It came to those who were in it for the long haul, who had a vision beyond the initial hype, and who were ready to build something that could stand the test of time. The lesson here? Do not just follow the rush, or hot trend—understand the game, know your lane, and play it smart. Because in the end, the real grinders are the ones who make it out on top.

Networking is not just for the suit-and-tie crowd; it is the lifeblood of success in blue-collar industries too. Do not get it twisted—who you know can be just as important as what you know. You can have all the skills in the world, but if you are not leveraging connections, you are leaving opportunities on the table. In this game, it is Network or Never. You must understand that building relationships, aligning with the right people, and positioning yourself within the right circles can be the difference between staying stagnant and skyrocketing your career. Let us break it down. Blue-collar industries are all about trust, reliability, and reputation. Guess what? Your reputation does not just get built on your work ethic alone; it is also built on the relationships you forge. When you are in the trenches, working shoulder-to-shoulder with your peers, your network becomes your safety net, your ladder to the next level, and sometimes even your shield from setbacks. In these industries, word of mouth is king. If you are not making moves to be part of the living conversation, you are playing a losing hand. But here is the thing—you cannot network effectively without being strategic about it. This is not about collecting business cards or shaking hands just for the sake of it. It is about understanding who you need to know, who can elevate your game, and who you can learn from. It is about building a network of people who will go to bat for you, who will bring you in on opportunities, and who will push you to be better. To do that, you have to be authentic, consistent, and intentional.

You have to show up, contribute, and be the kind of person others want in their corner. That means knowing your value, understanding the value of others, and being smart about how you leverage those relationships. Whether you're in construction, manufacturing, or any other blue-collar field, networking is your secret weapon, and it's not exclusive to white collar professionals only. Use it wisely, and there is no limit to how far you can go. The following quotes are not just words; they are principles to live by. Whether you are on the field, in the trenches, or leading a team, understanding the power of unity, teamwork, and Network is essential to success. In the world of blue-collar industries, where the grind is real, and every move counts, you cannot afford to go it alone. Surround yourself with the right people, build strong relationships, and never underestimate the power of a solid core network. That is not how you the secure victories…it is always strength in numbers.

"The strength of the team is each individual member. The strength of each member is the team."

— Phil Jackson

- Jackson led the Chicago Bulls and Los Angeles Lakers to multiple NBA championships, proving that teamwork, more than any individual talent, is what wins championships.

"If everyone is moving forward together, then success takes care of itself."

— Henry Ford

- Ford revolutionized the automobile industry not just with innovation but with a workforce that moved as one, proving that collective effort drives extraordinary success.

"It is amazing what you can accomplish if you do not care who gets the credit."

— Harry S. Truman

- the 33rd President of the United States knew that true leadership and teamwork are about focusing on the mission, not individual accolades.

"We must all hang together, or, most assuredly, we shall all hang separately."

— Benjamin Franklin

- This quote from the American Revolutionary War era underscores the critical importance of unity in the face of adversity.

"None of us is as smart as all of us."

— Ken Blanchard

- Blanchard, a management expert, emphasizes that collective intelligence and teamwork always outperform individual brilliance.

"Unity is strength... when there is teamwork and collaboration, wonderful things can be achieved."

— Mattie Stepanek

- This young poet and peace advocate understood that teamwork magnifies success, no matter the odds.

"The way a team plays determines its success. You may have the greatest bunch of individual stars in the world, but if they don't play together, the club won't be worth a dime."

— Babe Ruth

- The Sultan of Swat knew that even in baseball, the ultimate team sport, unity is what wins games, not just individual talent.

"One arrow alone can be easily broken but many arrows are indestructible."

— Genghis Khan

- The Mongol Empire did not become the largest contiguous empire in history without a deep understanding of the power of unity and collective strength.

"In union, there is strength."

— Aesop

- This ancient Greek storyteller taught us through his fables that unity is the foundation of resilience and power.

"Family is not an important thing. It's everything."

— Michael J. Fox

- Fox's words remind us that in life, whether in business or personal affairs, your family—those who support and stand by you—are your greatest asset and strength.

Betrayal and being overlooked can hit hard, no doubt. It is easy to get jaded when you have been burned by those you thought had your back. But here is the thing—holding onto that negativity can block you from ever getting a seat at the table, let alone an invite into that exclusive expansion circle. It is a tough pill to swallow, but the truth is, sometimes we are our own worst enemy. Teamwork is crucial, but before you think about what the team is doing, you must look hard in the mirror.

Ask yourself the real questions:

- Would I want to team up with me if the roles were reversed? Are you the kind of person you would want to rely on? It's easy to point fingers when things go south but flip the script.

- If you were someone else looking in, would you see yourself as an asset or a liability? That is a question only you can answer, and it requires brutal honesty. What do I bring to the table?

- If you did get the invite, what value are you adding? It is not just about showing up—it's about showing up ready to contribute. You must have something real to offer, something that makes the circle stronger. Because the truth is, nobody is looking for dead weight. They want players, not benchwarmers.

- Have I cultivated knowledge that sets me apart? In today's world, basic information is a dime a dozen. But non-typical, specialized knowledge? That is where the gold is. In other words, telling me something I do not know is the mantra of the landscape.

- Have you taken the time to dig deeper, to learn something unique that could benefit the whole team? If not, you are just blending in with the crowd, and that is not going to cut it when it comes to building powerful networks.

Look, being jaded is easy. It is a natural reaction to getting hurt. But if you let that jaded mindset, take root, you will miss opportunities that could change your life. It is not just about being invited into the circle; it is about being ready for it when the time comes. You must grind on yourself first, sharpen your own skills, and build your own values. That is how you make sure that when the opportunity does knock, you are not just ready to answer—you are ready to stand on it, and that is what makes a network solid.

PLAYBOOK #5

"KNOWING WHEN TO PIVOT: THE ART OF MOVING ON"

Now, let's get real about why it's so damn hard for highly skilled professionals to walk away from a toxic job or company. You'd think that with all the talent, experience, and expertise they've built up over the years, these folks would have no problem packing up and moving on. But the truth is, they're often the ones who stay the longest, grinding themselves down in environments that don't deserve them. There are some deep reasons why this happens. First off, it's that golden handcuff syndrome. When you're highly skilled, you're likely getting paid well. The salary, the benefits, the stock options—it all looks good on paper. But here's the catch: the higher the paycheck, the harder it is to leave, even when you know the place is toxic. It's a psychological trap. You start telling yourself that you've got too much to lose, that you won't find something better, or that the money makes it all worth it. But let me tell you, no amount of money is worth your peace of mind, your health, or your happiness. Also, let's not forget about the investment you've made. By the time you reach a certain level of expertise, you've poured years—maybe decades—into building your career. You've earned those degrees, certifications, and accolades. You've climbed the corporate ladder. So, the idea of walking away feels like you're throwing all that hard work out the window. But here's the thing: staying in a toxic environment isn't just a waste of your talent; it's a betrayal of everything you've worked for. You're not abandoning your investment by leaving; you're protecting it.

Another reason highly skilled professionals get stuck is fear of the unknown. Even with all that talent, it's scary to step into the unknown, especially when you've been at one company for years. There's a sense of security, even if it's false, in sticking with what you know, even when it's killing you. The fear of failure in a new role, or the anxiety of starting over, can paralyze you into staying put. But here's the harsh reality: every day you stay in that toxic environment, you're delaying your own growth, your own success, and your own happiness. You're stunting your potential because you're afraid of what's on the other side of that door. And then there's the loyalty factor. You've built relationships, maybe even friendships, with your colleagues. You've got a sense of duty, of responsibility to the team or the company. But let's keep it real loyalty is a two-way street, and if the company isn't loyal to you, if they're draining you dry and giving nothing back, that loyalty is misplaced. It's time to be loyal to yourself, to your future, and to your own well-being. Because at the end of the day, the company will replace you in a heartbeat, but you can't replace the time and energy you've lost. Now, let's talk data. At the time of writing this book, according to the American Psychological Association, workplace stress costs American companies over $500 billion annually and is linked to 120,000 deaths each year.

You think that doesn't apply to highly skilled professionals? Think again. The more skilled you are, the more responsibilities you take on, and the more pressure you face. The World Health Organization has classified burnout as an occupational phenomenon, and research shows that it's especially prevalent among high-achievers—people who pour everything into their work and end up paying the price with their mental and physical health. So why do they stay? It's that toxic mix of fear, financial security, misplaced loyalty, and the psychological investment of years spent building a career.

Harsh truth: no job, no paycheck, no title is worth sacrificing your health, your peace of mind, or your future. Highly skilled or not, you've got to recognize when it's time to pivot, when it's time to protect what you've built by finding a place that values you, respects you, and lets you thrive. You're not just a cog in a machine, and you're not here to be used up and thrown away. You've got the skills, the talent, and the drive to succeed anywhere. Don't let fear or a false sense of security keep you trapped in a place that's killing your potential. Know your worth, and when the time comes, don't be afraid to walk away. That's how you truly build—and that's how you avoid being destroyed."

One of the hardest lessons you will ever learn in your grind: knowing when to move on. My mentor, 'R.B.,' always used to say, 'Death by a thousand cuts.' It is that slow, agonizing drain of your energy, your passion, and your potential in a toxic or unhealthy environment. You might not even realize it at first, but every day, you are losing a little bit more of yourself until there is nothing left. And all for what? A paycheck that does not match your worth. A job that makes you miserable? That is when you must wake up and recognize that all money is not good. Remember, everything is related to everything, and business is simply Pimps and hoes at the end of the day. Think about it; the job/business/corporation is the pimp looking for those they cannot exploit for expanded financial gains, whether it is short or prolonged. The Pimp/corporation does not care or mind when a bitch/employee leaves, because like all business, they understand it is all "cop n blow," meaning you are going to lose a hoe, even your best hoe. There is an unwritten understanding that at some point they will wise up or become too burnt out to perform at an elevated level for that pimp/corporation. You have seen what happens to the high performer types with the built-in motor for success. The "automatic types," that clock-in and smash all given task and goals present to them types. The business/pimp loves these bottom bitch types. They help relay the company/pimp vision to the other teammates/stablemates and set the tone for the ideal culture. The business/pimp knows deep down they will not get maximum effort from each employee/hoe, but that bottom bitch employee will at least keep the trend moving fwd... Corporations play the long game forever, meaning the plan on attrition, mutinies, disheveled attitudes, rebels, and complaints, especially from that outstanding bottom bitch at some point. They plan on that outstanding bottom bitch employee clocking out one day and never coming back, and like a pimp, they will have an ice-cold poker face the whole time.

A good pimp will put the bottom bitch with the rookie of the year type hoe, the slightly younger but slightly green hoe. The instruct the (bottom bitch/go-to employee) to teach the (green hoe/new hire with promise) everything they know and bring them up to speed and on program.

Corporations have created politically correct jargon for this street tactic, and they call it succession planning. Succession planning involves identifying and developing internal employees with the potential to fill key leadership positions within the organization in the future (sound familiar). It ensures that there is a plan in place to maintain business continuity when key employees leave or retire. "Legacy planning" is a broader term that can include succession planning but also encompasses the impact you want to leave behind, such as the long-term goals, values, and mission of the company or your personal legacy within it. However, when specifically referring to preparing someone to replace you in your role, "succession planning" is the most accurate term. Like I said before, its all related at the end of the day.

Their (management/pimp) bigger than you, the company (the game) is bigger than you, the money is bigger than you, therefore they will not show an ounce of frustration at your departure, they must be God all the way. See, here is the game corporations play—they see you as a battery. You have energy, skills, and drive, and they are going to drain every bit of it out of you until you are nothing but a husk. And whose fault is that? It is yours because you signed up for it. You signed that application, put on that uniform, and agreed to follow rules you had no hand in making. You agreed to be another cog in the machine, and now the machine's chewing you up and spitting you out. Here is where it gets real: you have a choice. You do not have to stay in a place that is killing your spirit. You do not have to keep clocking in to a job that makes you feel like less of a man every single day. Just because you signed up does not mean you are locked in for life. It is on you to recognize when it is time to pivot, to make the move that is right for you, and to reclaim your power. Think about it—how many times have you taken orders from someone who can't even run their own life, but they have you jumping through hoops at work? They do not care about you, your future, or your well-being. They are just playing a role, exercising their little bit of power in the only place they can. But outside of those corporate walls, they're are nobody. And here you are, letting them dictate your day, your mood, your life. Let me tell you something: you're not a battery. You're not here to be used up and discarded. You're here to build something real, something that lasts, and something that reflects your true value. And sometimes, that means you've got to know when to walk away. It is not about quitting; it's about recognizing when the game is rigged against you and finding a new path where you can thrive. So, if you are stuck in a situation where every day feels like another cut, bleeding you dry, it's time to ask yourself: Is this what you signed up for? Or is it time to pivot, to find a new opportunity that respects your skillset, your hustle, and your potential? Because at the end of the day, no one is going to look out for you but you. That means knowing when to move on, to take control of your life, and to stop letting others dictate your destiny.

Remember, all money is not good money. Your time, your energy, your life—they're worth more than a paycheck. So, make the move when you need to. Don't let yourself be drained to nothing. You're better than that. You're built to build, not to be destroyed. Staying in a toxic environment is not just a bad move—it is a slow death. You are not just sacrificing your health, your career, and your relationships; you are sacrificing your future. Recognize the signs, and when it's time to move on, do it without hesitation. That is how you protect yourself, your potential, and your legacy from the following:

- **Physical Breakdown:** Staying in a toxic environment will eventually take a toll on your body. Chronic stress leads to high blood pressure, heart disease, and a weakened immune system. You're risking long-term health issues that could haunt you for the rest of your life.

- **Mental and Emotional Burnout:** Over time, the constant pressure, negativity, and lack of fulfillment will wear you down mentally. Depression, anxiety, and burnout are real outcomes. You'll find yourself dreading each day, losing interest in things you used to love, and feeling trapped in a cycle you can't escape.

- **Erosion of Self-Worth:** The longer you stay, the more your confidence erodes. You start to believe the lies—that you're only worth what the company says you are, that you're stuck, that you're not good enough to find something better. This leads to a downward spiral where you stop pushing for more and settle for less.

- **Stalled Career Growth:** In a toxic environment, your career growth hits a ceiling. You're too consumed with surviving the day-to-day to focus on advancing. Your skills stagnate, your network shrinks, and opportunities pass you by. Before you know it, years have gone by, and you're in the same spot, watching others move ahead.

- **Strained Personal Relationships:** Toxic work environments do not just stay at work—they bleed into your personal life. You bring stress, frustration, and exhaustion home, which strains your relationships with family and friends. Over time, this could lead to isolation, broken relationships, and a deep sense of loneliness.

- **Financial Instability:** If the toxicity pushes you to the edge and you leave without a plan, you could find yourself in financial turmoil. Quitting on a whim without a safety net can lead to unemployment, debt, and the struggle to make ends meet. The irony is that the financial security you stayed for might end up being your downfall.

- **Lost Time and Regret:** The worst part is looking back and realizing how much time you've lost time you'll never get back. The years spent in a toxic environment could have been spent building something better, learning new skills, or enjoying life. The regret of lost time is heavy and can leave a permanent mark on your soul.

- **Permanent Damage to Your Reputation:** In some cases, staying too long in a toxic environment can damage your professional reputation. If the company has a bad rep, or if you start to reflect the negativity around you, it could make it harder to find new opportunities. Your name could be associated with failure, making it difficult to pivot to something better.

Please understand that this playbook doesn't just apply to career types, but it directly applies to my renegade entrepreneur types. One of the hardest things for any entrepreneur to face is the idea that something they've believed in—even built their business around—just isn't working anymore. But let me tell you, clinging to a philosophy or an idea that no longer serves you isn't just a bad strategy; it's a straight-up liability. It's like trying to drive forward while staring in the rearview mirror. If you're not willing to adapt, evolve, and sometimes outright abandon what's not working, you're setting yourself up for failure. There's data to back this up. According to a study by Harvard Business School, 75% of venture-backed startups fail. Why? One of the biggest reasons is a lack of adaptability—entrepreneurs get so attached to their original idea or philosophy that they refuse to pivot when the market, their customers, or even their own business needs change. They keep pouring time, energy, and money into something that's sinking because they're too stubborn to admit it's not working. That's not just bad business; that's ego-driven self-destruction, or like my grandfather put it to me when he witnessed me struggling with a business idea...don't keep putting good money after bad money. When you're locked-in on the grind, it's easy to get attached to the philosophies and or trends that got you started. Perhaps, it's a certain approach to leadership, a specific business model, or a rigid belief in how things 'should' be done.

Harsh truth: what got you here will not necessarily get you there. The market evolves, technology advances, customer expectations shift, and if you are not willing to evolve with them, you are going to get left behind.

Real-life modern-day examples Prove this fact. Think about Blockbuster. They had the chance to buy Netflix for $50 million back in the early 2000s, but they passed because they were too attached to their brick-and-mortar philosophy. They could not see the future that streaming represented. Fast forward, and Netflix is now worth over $200 billion (about $620 per person in the US) while Blockbuster is a memory. Why? Because Blockbuster couldn't let go of a philosophy that no longer served them. But it's not just about recognizing when an idea is outdated; it's about having the courage to act on that recognition. A lot of entrepreneurs know deep down when something isn't working, but they are afraid to make the change. They fear uncertainty, potential failure, or the loss of what they have built. But here is the thing: inaction is real failure. You're not just risking your current business—you are risking your entire future. Who are you trying to please or impress, because if that person is not you, reevaluate the reasoning for starting and or continuing your pursuits. Research from the University of Chicago shows that entrepreneurs who pivot, who aren't afraid to change direction, when necessary, are significantly more successful overall. They are the ones who survive, who grow, and who thrive, again putting emphasis on the long play, and proper alignment with time. They understand that entrepreneurship isn't about sticking to one idea: it's about constantly evolving, learning, and adapting to the environment around you. So, why is it important to know when to give up a philosophy or idea? Because your success as an entrepreneur depends on your ability to recognize when something isn't serving you anymore and to have the guts to pivot. It's about being real with yourself—knowing that holding on to the past because it's comfortable or familiar isn't going to get you where you want to go.

It is about protecting your business, your future, and your growth by being willing to let go of what is holding you back. You must be ruthless with your growth. If something isn't working, cut it loose. Do not let outdated ideas or philosophies drag you down. Be willing to evolve, adapt, and sometimes destroy what you have built to create something even better. That is the mindset of a true entrepreneur. Let us break this down with some real data and examples. Staying in a toxic work environment isn't just bad for your mental health—it's a slow poison that seeps into every part of your life, and the numbers back it up. Research shows that prolonged exposure to toxic work environments significantly increases the risk of anxiety, depression, and burnout. According to a 2020 study published in the Journal of Occupational Health Psychology, employees trapped in high-stress, low-control jobs are 2.5 times more likely to develop depressive symptoms than those in healthier work environments. And we are not just talking about a difficult day here and there. We are talking about a constant, grinding pressure that eats away at your well-being over time. Think about the "emotional exhaustion" you hear about in industrial research. It is a clinical term, but what it really means is that you are drained—mentally, emotionally, and physically. You have nothing left to give because the job has sucked it all out of you.

A study from the American Psychological Association found that 75% of workers who reported feeling emotionally exhausted also reported decreased job performance and a significant drop in life satisfaction. That's not a coincidence—it's a direct result of staying in a toxic situation for too long. Take the concept of "presenteeism," where you're physically at work, but your mind is checked out. You're going through the motions, but the passion, the drive—it's all gone. A 2018 study in the Harvard Business Review found that presenteeism costs U.S. companies over $150 billion annually in lost productivity. But beyond the dollars and cents, it's costing you your mental health. Staying in a job where you feel undervalued, overworked, or outright mistreated doesn't just affect your work; it bleeds into your personal life, damaging relationships and eroding your self-esteem. Let's look at real-life examples. In the manufacturing sector, a study conducted by the National Institute for Occupational Safety and Health found that workers exposed to hostile work environments—constant criticism, unreasonable demands, lack of support—showed higher rates of cardiovascular disease. This isn't just psychological; it's physiological. Stress manifests in your body, raising your blood pressure, messing with your sleep, and weakening your immune system. Or consider the telecommunications industry. A report from the World Health Organization highlighted how employees in high-pressure, low-reward environments are more prone to chronic stress, leading to higher rates of substance abuse as a coping mechanism. That's the kind of downward spiral that's hard to escape once it starts. The bottom line? Staying too long in a toxic situation isn't just bad for your career—it's bad for your health, your happiness, and your future. You've got to recognize the signs and have the courage to move on. The longer you stay, the more damage you're doing, and no job is worth that. Your health, your mental clarity, and your sense of purpose are too valuable to sacrifice on the altar of a toxic work environment. Let me tell you something real: nobody is coming to save you. You've heard that phrase, right? It's a wake-up call, but most folks miss the point. See, no one is going to rescue you from your own mess, and nobody's risking their peace to fix your chaos. That's why you need to trust your gut and know when it's time to bounce away from a toxic situation. You can't point fingers at a job for keeping you "just over broke," and you can't blame the corporate grind for draining your spirit day in and day out. That's how you end up a living corpse, going through the motions but dead inside.

Harsh truth: every job is a mission behind enemy lines. Deep down, you know that gig isn't yours to keep. Think about it—if you really owned it, how could they fire or lay you off without a second thought? You've got no real control because it's not your business; it's just your turn until they decide your time's up. I've seen it happen over and over in my 15 years in aviation—corporate meat grinders chewing up vibrant souls and spitting out empty shells. What about that "buy-in speech" they give you on day one. You know the drill: "I need you to buy in," "treat this place like it's yours," "take ownership." It's all psychological warfare, designed to make you feel like you've got a stake in the game. But it's a trap. They want you to throw yourself on the grenade when things go sideways, all for the company's bottom line. The truth is nothing about that setup is meant to elevate you. If you start climbing too high, they know you'll eventually outgrow the grind and leave for something better. That's not in their interest.

I'm not here to bash big business. I'm just holding up a mirror. The stress, the burnout, the declining health—it's all on you. You signed up for this, and you stayed too long. Pursue those big dreams, but don't ever forget: a job is just a job. It's a tool to get you where you want to go, but if you hang on too long, it'll turn you on. The longer you stay in the wrong situation, the more it'll wear you down. Recognize that trend and have the courage to make a move before it is too late.

PLAYBOOK #6

"CERTIFIED TO SUCCEED: THE POWER OF PROFESSIONAL CREDENTIALS"

No matter what, make sure you have that paper behind your name, otherwise you'll be hit out here in this life, my uncle Mr. Rashid would say to me during the scorching summer days when I would spend the weekends with my cousins during summer and spring breaks. Mr. Rashid was the owner/operator of P.S.R construction company. He moved from his home country of Jamacia during the 1980's and came to Detroit with his work ethic and skillset to build a better life. Mr. Rashid was a man of few words, because frankly he did not have to run his mouth as his presence spoke volumes. He was a master carpenter/journeyman, a certification that many in the field never bother pursuing, because frankly, many are just content with earning a paycheck working for another person, but this was not my uncle's path. Mr. Rashid has shown interest in my life and or goals whenever I had the pleasure of being in his presence. Yes, this man was not my father, but in many instances, he treated me like one of his own. Immediately after greeting him, he'd ask; "so what are you working on Tony? I'd shrug my shoulders and give him a passive answer like; "I'm trying to figure it out uncle". Of course I'd be hit with a blunt rebuke, something to the effect of; Don't waste your time trying to figure such things out, you need to develop a skill that's going to keep your from being poor and homeless, you'll figure out that other stuff later, when you have a full belly of food. He taught me the value of work ethic, and tangible skills. Mr. Rashid taught me how to install windows, painting, and the basics of framing, along with gutter crimping and installation during those summers I had the privilege to work as an apprentice. Witnessing my cousins working like well-oiled machines, while laughing and joking with one another under the blazing sun from sunup to sundown always blew my mind and contributed to my own work ethic and character development. Overall, the key takeaway I gathered from my uncle is…When you have skills that solve problems, you'll never go broke or hungry. Mr. Rashid's character, poise, stoic demeanor, and willingness to pass down his knowledge truly set him apart, and I'm forever grateful to have been mentored by him throughout my youth.

When it comes to grinding in the blue-collar world, you either got the tools, or you don't. But here's the thing—tools aren't just wrenches, hammers, or the machines you operate. No, one of the sharpest tools you can have in your arsenal is a certification, a professional credential that says, "I'm not just about the grind, I'm about mastering it." It's about being undeniable, making sure that when you walk into a room—whether it's a job site, a boardroom, or an interview—you're bringing more than just sweat equity. You are bringing receipts, proof that you have put in the work to know your craft inside and out. In today's world, paper speaks.

That certification, that credential, is your ticket to not just staying in the game, but to leveling up. It is the difference between being just another worker on the line and being the go-to expert, everyone turns to when the stakes are high. It is about leveraging that knowledge and those skills to elevate not only your career, but personal elevation to make sure you are not just clocking in and out with a graveyard corporation but moving forward, climbing higher, and securing the bag in a flexible way. Think about it—how many times have you seen someone get passed over for a promotion, not because they could not do the job, but because they did not have the credentials? We have all been there, watching someone less skilled slide into a position because they had that extra piece of paper. That is the game, though, and if you want to win, you must play it smartly. Getting certified is not about learning; it is about positioning yourself as the top contender, the one who is ready to take on the toughest challenges and come out on top. Let's not get it twisted, certifications are not just for white-collar folks. Whether you're in welding, plumbing, aviation, or any skilled trade, having that certification under your belt is like carrying a sword in a battlefield. It's a weapon that gives you an edge, that sets you apart in a competitive industry where everyone is hustling to make their mark. So, if you are serious about success, if you're committed to building or destroying whatever is in your way, it's time to get certified, because in the grind of life, credentials are your currency, and those who have them rule the game. I'm not telling you to run out here and become a certification whore, not at all. You must prioritize which certifications can and will give the greatest leverage along your journey. Truth be told, many individuals get certifications, licenses, and degrees just to finger wave. Self-improvement, without a clear target in mind, becomes "stat-padding-masturbation". You are only doing it for self-pleasure, and pseudo bragging rights, throwing a party inside of an empty room. Let's break down why that piece of paper—whether it's a degree, a certification, or both—can be the key to unlocking a whole new level of earning potential. In the grind, everyone is working hard, but not everyone is getting paid the same. That is where credentials come into play, and they play a significant role in determining whether you are just surviving or truly thriving.

The Degree Advantage

First off, let us talk about degrees. It is no secret that in many industries, having a degree can put you on a different pay scale altogether. According to the latest data, workers with a bachelor's degree typically earn about 66% more than those with only a high school diploma. That is not a small gap—that is the difference between living paycheck to paycheck and being able to build some real wealth over time. For example, the median annual salary for someone with a bachelor's degree is around $55,000, while for those with just a high school diploma, it hovers closer to $33,000. Understand, it does not stop at the bachelor's level. Advanced degrees—like master's, PhDs, and professional degrees—push that earning potential even higher. We are talking six figures and beyond, especially in specialized fields like engineering, healthcare, or finance. Degrees open doors, and in many cases, they put you in rooms you would not even know existed without that education backing you up.

The Certification Edge

Now, let's shift gears to certifications. While a degree might be a long-term investment, certifications are the high-impact tools you can use to boost your earning potential more quickly. In some trades, a certification can mean the difference between making $50,000 a year and pulling in $80,000 or more. That's no exaggeration. For instance, a certified welder can earn up to $35 per hour, compared to $18 per hour for an uncertified welder. That is almost double the pay for the same work, but with the added expertise and trust that comes with being certified. The same goes for fields like IT, healthcare, and project management. Take IT, for example—having certifications like CompTIA, Cisco, or AWS can increase your salary by 20% or more compared to your uncertified peers. In project management, having a PMP (Project Management Professional) certification can boost your pay by nearly 25%. In healthcare, a certified medical coder earns an average of $64,000 annually, while their uncertified counterparts might bring home around $40,000.

The Pay Gap Reality

So, what's the reality of the pay gap? It's clear: credentials pay off. Workers with degrees and certifications not only earn more, but they also have better job security, more opportunities for advancement, and are often considered for leadership roles over those without credentials. The pay gap can be stark—sometimes as much as 50%—which translates into tens of thousands of dollars more per year. Over a career, that gap can add up to hundreds of thousands, if not millions, of dollars in lost income for those without credentials.

Why It Matters

Overall, the pay gap between credentialed and non-credentialed workers isn't about money. It's about leverage. It's about positioning yourself in a way that allows you to command respect, negotiate better deals, and move up in your career faster than someone who's just going through the motions. The bottom line? If you want to maximize your earning potential and utterly secure your financial future, getting those credentials—whether through a degree, a certification, or both—isn't just a clever idea; it's a necessity. Investing in yourself through education and certification is one of the smartest moves you can make in today's economy. It's not just about keeping up; it's about staying ahead, making sure that when opportunities arise, you're not just in the room—you're at the head of the table. Because when you bring that level of knowledge and proof of expertise, there's no limit to how far you can go in the grind of life.

When it comes to negotiating power and leverage, your credentials are like heavy artillery in a battlefield. The more you have, the stronger your position. Whether negotiating a salary, a promotion, or even a contract, having those degrees and certifications in your arsenal means not just asking—you are demanding, and there is a difference. Let us be real: In any negotiation, it is about what you bring to the table.

When you have the credentials to back up your experience, you are not coming empty-handed. You come with receipts that prove the worth of every dollar you're asking for, and then some. Employers know that certified and educated workers are not just clocking in—they're bringing value, reducing risk, and elevating the standards of the organization. That's power. For instance, say you're in a job interview, and you've got that certification or degree that's directly relevant to the role. Suddenly, the conversation is not about whether you're qualified—it's about how much they're willing to pay to get you on board. You've shifted the dynamics because your credentials put you in control. You're the one who decides if the offer is good enough, not the other way around. That is leverage. And let's talk about when you're already in a job. Suppose you've been killing it at work, but you're ready for the next level. If you've got certifications that prove you've mastered new skills or if you've earned a degree while working full-time, you've got a solid case to push for that raise or promotion. You're showing your employer that you're committed to growth and that you've got the credentials to back it up. They know that if they don't reward you, someone else will. Again, that's leverage. Leverage is all about positioning. The more you bring to the table, the more you can negotiate from a position of strength. You're not just another worker—

they cannot just replace you with someone off the street. You've got the knowledge, the skills, and the proof in the form of credentials. That makes you valuable, and when you're valuable, you are in demand. When you are in demand, you control the conversation. Without credentials, you are at the mercy of the market. But with them, you're the one setting the terms. We're not begging for a raise; but you are simply justifying why you deserve it. You're not asking for a promotion; you're proving why you're the best choice. This is the mindset you've got to have. In the game of life, credentials are your leverage, and the smart player uses every ounce of leverage they have to get ahead. So, when you are grinding, remember this: Knowledge isn't just power—it's negotiating power. In this world, that's the kind of power that can change your life.

Something that does not get enough attention: The connection between your credentials, your skills, and your mental health. When you've got tangible skills and certifications backing you up, you're not just stacking paper—you're building a fortress around your mental well-being. The Mental Edge of Being Certified Research shows that those with certifications, degrees, or specialized skills are more likely to report higher levels of job satisfaction and lower levels of stress. Why? Because when you've got something to show your grind, you've got options. You're not stuck in a dead-end job, praying for the next paycheck. You know that if things get bad, you've got the credentials to walk away and find something better. That kind of security is priceless—it's mental armor.

A study from the National Bureau of Economic Research found that workers with higher levels of education and specialized skills report better mental health outcomes than those without. This is not about having a diploma to hang on the wall; it's about the confidence that comes with knowing you're capable, qualified, and in demand. You walk differently when you know you're valuable. That confidence spills over into how you handle stress, how you approach challenges, and even how you see yourself. The Trap of Being Unskilled and Uncredentialed On the other side, let us talk about what happens when you do not have that foundation. When you're working without any certifications or specialized skills, you're constantly playing defense. You're worrying about job security, stressing over whether you'll be the next one cut during layoffs, and doubting your ability to move up in life. All that eats away at your mental health. Research published in The Lancet Psychiatry found that workers without formal education or specialized skills are more likely to experience anxiety, depression, and even substance abuse. When you don't have that piece of paper backing you up, you're more likely to feel stuck, undervalued, and overwhelmed. You don't see a way out, and that kind of hopelessness can destroy your mental health. The Power of Choice What credentials really give you is choice. And choice is a powerful thing when it comes to mental health. When you know you've got the skills to pivot, to take your talents elsewhere, if necessary, you're not just surviving—you're thriving.

You are not tied to a toxic environment because you fear what's out there. You're making moves because you know you've got the credentials to land on your feet, no matter what. Having skills and certifications means you're playing offense, not defense. You're building a life on your terms, not just reacting to what life throws at you. That proactive approach doesn't just boost your career—it safeguards your mental health. You are not just grinding; you're grinding with purpose, and that makes all the difference. The Takeaway at the end of the day, the connection between your skills, your credentials, and your mental health is undeniable. When you invest in yourself through education and certification, you're not just boosting your income—you're fortifying your mind. You are building a foundation of confidence, security, and choice. Without those things, you're at the mercy of the world, and that's a dangerous place to be. In the game of life, you can't afford to be unskilled or uncredentialed. The stakes are too high, and your mental health is too important. So, keep grinding, keep learning, and keep building those credentials. Because when you do, you're not just leveling up your career—you're leveling up your life.

Let us get into the certifications and licenses that are set to dominate the next decade. We are talking about the kind of credentials that do not just get you in the door—they kick the door down and put you in control. Whether you are in the trades, tech, or any other blue-collar industry, these are the certifications that are going to separate the grinders from the rest of the pack.

1. **Cybersecurity Certifications (CISSP, CEH, CISM)**

   In a world where data is more valuable than gold, cybersecurity is the fortress that protects it. The demand for cybersecurity experts is skyrocketing, with the need for certifications like CISSP (Certified Information Systems Security Professional), CEH (Certified Ethical Hacker), and CISM (Certified Information Security Manager) expected to grow by 32% by 2030. These certifications are not just nice to have—they are essential in a world where cyber threats are the new frontier of warfare.

2. **Project Management Professional (PMP)**

   No matter what the industry is, someone must keep the trains running on time. That is where the PMP certification comes in. With businesses facing tighter deadlines and budgets, the need for skilled project managers is expected to surge. Holding a PMP can set you apart as the one who can handle the pressure and deliver results, making this certification one of the most sought-after by 2030.

3. Renewable Energy Technician Certification

As the world shifts towards sustainable energy, the demand for professionals who can install and maintain renewable energy systems is going to explode. Certifications in solar, wind, and other renewable energy technologies will be in high demand, with growth projected at 52% by 2030. This is your chance to get in on the ground floor of a booming industry.

4. Healthcare IT Certifications (CPHIMS, RHIA)

The intersection of healthcare and technology is where the future is being built. Certifications like CPHIMS (Certified Professional in Healthcare Information and Management Systems) and RHIA (Registered Health Information Administrator) are set to be game changers, especially as telemedicine and digital health records become the norm. This field is expected to grow by 28% by 2030, making these credentials highly valuable.

5. AWS Certified Solutions Architect

Cloud computing is not just a trend; it is the future of IT. As more companies move their operations to the cloud, certifications like AWS Certified Solutions Architect are going to be in high demand. The cloud computing industry is expected to grow by 23% by 2030, and having this certification will position you as a key player in this rapidly expanding field.

6. Certified Data Analyst (CAP, Google Data Analytics)

Data is the new oil, and those who can mine, refine, and analyze it will control the future. Certifications like CAP (Certified Analytics Professional) and Google Data Analytics are essential for anyone looking to make their mark in the world of big data. With an expected growth rate of 26% by 2030, data analytics is a field that is only going up.

7. **Licensed Practical Nurse (LPN)**

The healthcare industry is always in demand, but with an aging population, the need for skilled nurses is becoming very high. The LPN license is projected to be one of the most in-demand certifications in the healthcare sector, with job growth expected to increase by 25% by 2030. This isn't just a job—it's a career that saves lives and brings stability.

8. **Certified Electrician**

As the world becomes more dependent on electricity—whether it's for charging electric vehicles or powering smart homes—the need for certified electricians is going to soar. With an expected job growth of 20% by 2030, becoming a certified electrician is not just a smart move—it's a powerful one.

9. **Artificial Intelligence and Machine Learning Certifications**

AI is not the future; it is the present, and it's transforming every industry. Certifications in AI and machine learning from institutions like Coursera, Google, or IBM will be highly sought after, with demand expected to grow by 35% by 2030. This is the forefront of technology, and having these credentials will put you at the forefront.

10. **Welding Certifications (CWI, CWE)**

In the manufacturing and construction industries, welding is the backbone that holds everything together. Certified Welders (CWI, CWE) are in short supply, but the demand is set to increase by 14% by 2030. Whether it is building infrastructure or maintaining industrial equipment, certified welders are going to be indispensable. Wrapping It Up These certifications are not about checking a box—they are about positioning yourself to be indispensable in the years to come. The world is changing fast, and the people who are going to thrive are the ones who are prepared. Whether you are looking to secure a better paycheck, gain more negotiating power, or simply future proof of your career, these certifications are your ticket to the top. So, keep grinding, keep learning, and make sure you are ready to capitalize on the opportunities that are coming. Because when you are certified, you are not just ready—you become unstoppable.

11. Aerospace Certifications/Licenses

When it comes to the aerospace industry, having the right credentials is not just a formality—it is the difference between being another name on the roster and being someone who can command respect, higher pay, and more opportunities. Credentials like Non-Destructive Testing (NDT) certifications and an Airframe and Powerplant (A&P) license are among the most sought-after in the field, and the demand for professionals holding these qualifications is on a steep incline. Why These Credentials Matter Non-Destructive Testing (NDT) Certifications are crucial in aerospace for ensuring the structural integrity of aircraft without causing damage. NDT technicians are the unsung heroes who make sure every weld, rivet, and composite material can withstand the extreme stresses of flight. As aircraft become more complex with advanced materials and designs, the demand for skilled NDT professionals is set to grow significantly. The global aerospace NDT market is projected to reach $1.6 billion by 2030, reflecting the critical need for these skills. Airframe and Powerplant (A&P) License holders are the backbone of aircraft maintenance. This license allows you to work on every part of an aircraft except for avionics, ensuring it is airworthy and meets all safety standards. With the continued expansion of the global fleet—Boeing estimates needing 769,000 new maintenance technicians by 2038—the demand for A&P mechanics is only going up. This is not about meeting a quota; it is about ensuring that the planes carrying millions of passengers each day are safe and reliable. Demand

Aerospace High Drivers: (Aging Aircraft Fleets)

As commercial airlines and military fleets age, the need for certified professionals to inspect, maintain, and overhaul these aircraft is increasing. This creates a continuous demand for both NDT technicians and A&P mechanics.

Stringent Safety Regulations:

Aerospace is one of the most heavily regulated industries in the world. Meeting the rigorous standards set by agencies like the FAA means that only those with the proper credentials can perform critical inspections and repairs. This creates a high barrier to entry and ensures that those with the right qualifications are in constant demand.

New Aircraft Production:

With companies like Boeing and Airbus ramping up production of new models, the need for professionals to ensure these aircraft meet safety and performance standards from the production floor to the runway is skyrocketing.

Technological Advancements:

As aircraft technology evolves, so does the complexity of the maintenance required. Advanced materials like carbon fiber and composites, along with more sophisticated avionics, mean that NDT and A&P professionals need to be more skilled than ever. Employers are looking for those who not only work with current technologies but also adapt to new ones. Career Impact Having an NDT certification or an A&P license not only makes you more employable but also gives you leverage. You are not just another employee; you are a specialist in a field that is crucial to the safety and efficiency of an industry worth trillions of dollars. This kind of leverage translates into better pay, more job security, and greater opportunities for advancement.

According to the Bureau of Labor Statistics, the median salary for aircraft and avionics mechanics and technicians is around $66,000, but those with advanced certifications or specialized skills can command much higher salaries. Moreover, the ability to work on the most advanced aircraft in the world opens doors to positions in both commercial and military sectors, globally. In aerospace, credentials are your ticket to the big leagues. Whether it is an NDT certification or an A&P license, these qualifications place you in high demand in an industry that is both expanding and evolving. The future of aerospace is bright, and those who are certified are the ones who will be in the pilot's seat, steering their careers toward greater heights.

Creating separation in the workplace—especially in the career hierarchy—is not about climbing the ladder or securing that next promotion. It is a psychological game as much as it is a strategic one. When you deliberately set yourself apart from your peers, you are not just marking your territory; you are carving out a mental space where you can thrive, innovate, and lead.

The Power of Psychological Separation

1. **Enhanced Self-Efficacy**

   When you set yourself apart through skills, credentials, or sheer work ethic, you create a powerful sense of self-efficacy—the belief in your ability to execute and achieve goals. Research consistently shows that higher self-efficacy is linked to better job performance, increased job satisfaction, and lower stress levels. It is like putting on mental armor; the more confident you are in your abilities, the more resilient you become in the face of challenges. This separation also fosters a growth mindset, making you more likely to seek out new opportunities and embrace challenges as they come.

2. Reduced Job Stress

When you are constantly in the thick of competition, battling it out at the same level as everyone else, stress becomes an everyday companion. But when you create separation—by developing niche skills, gaining unique certifications, or simply outperforming your peers—you elevate yourself above the fray. According to a study published in the Journal of Occupational Health Psychology, employees who perceive themselves as being in a higher organizational status report lower levels of job-related stress and burnout. This makes sense because when you are not constantly looking over your shoulder, you can focus more on your work and less on office politics.

3. Improved Job Satisfaction

It is no secret that those who feel in control of their careers tend to be more satisfied with their jobs. Creating separation gives you that control. You are not just another cog in the machine; you are an essential piece of the puzzle. This autonomy is linked to higher levels of job satisfaction, as shown in research from the Harvard Business Review. People who feel they have a unique role to play are more engaged and committed to their work, leading to better performance and greater career success.

Data-Driven Insights

1. Higher Career Satisfaction

A study by Gallup found that employees who perceive themselves as having higher status or standing within their organization report significantly higher levels of career satisfaction. This is because they have more access to resources, greater control over their work, and more opportunities for advancement. When you create separation, you put yourself in a position where you are not just working a job—you are building a career.

2. Enhanced Professional Relationships

Creating separation does not mean alienating yourself from your peers; in fact, it can have the opposite effect. When you stand out for your skills and contributions, others are more likely to seek you out for collaboration, mentorship, and leadership. This enhances your professional network, which is a critical factor in long-term career success. A study by the Center for Creative Leadership found that strong professional networks are directly correlated with career advancement and job satisfaction.

3. Long-Term Mental Health Benefits

Longitudinal research from the American Psychological Association suggests that individuals who achieve higher career status tend to report better mental health outcomes over time. This is partly due to the increased control and autonomy they have in their work, which reduces feelings of helplessness and stress. Creating separation not only boosts your career but also contributes to your overall well-being.

Conclusion:

The Strategic Advantage Creating separation in the workplace is a strategic move that pays off in multiple ways. It enhances your self-efficacy, reduces job-related stress, and improves job satisfaction. Beyond that, it strengthens your professional network and contributes to better long-term mental health. In the end, those who create separation are not just surviving the workplace—they are thriving in it. The psychological benefits are clear: when you stand out, you stand tall, and when you stand tall, you set yourself up for success. So, as you navigate your career, remember that separation is not about getting ahead—it is about building a foundation where you can be your best, mentally and professionally.

PLAYBOOK #7

"STEM-ING AHEAD: BREAKING GROUND IN SCIENCE AND TECH"

Listen up because this is where the game changes. The world is shifting, and the opportunities are ripe for taking in STEM—Science, Technology, Engineering, and Mathematics. But let us not get it twisted; this is not for the guys in lab coats or the computer geeks in hoodies. STEM is the new frontier, and if you are an industrial athlete—a grinder, a hustler, someone who knows how to put in work—then this is your invitation to step up and break ground in a field that is not just lucrative but also transformative. First, understand that STEM is where the future is being built. Every innovation, every breakthrough that is pushing the world forward is happening in these fields. We are talking about the technology that is revolutionizing industries, the engineering that is building tomorrow's infrastructure, the mathematics that is driving data and analytics, and the science that is solving the world's biggest challenges. These are not just careers; they are missions. If you are ready to grind, the rewards are monumental. The Playing Field Has Changed in the old days, you might have thought that the only way to make it big was to either climb the corporate ladder or get your hands dirty on the factory floor. But today, the playing field has changed. STEM offers a path where you can not only carve out a lucrative career but also be part of something bigger. You are not just working a job; you are contributing to advancements that have the power to change the world. And the best part? The demand for skilled professionals in these fields is only going up. Here is the deal: Companies in every sector—whether it is aerospace, automotive, telecommunications, or even agriculture—are on the hunt for people who understand the details of technology and innovation. They need problem solvers, critical thinkers, and individuals who can take theoretical knowledge and turn it into real-world solutions. And this is where you come in. Your work ethic, your ability to grind through challenges, and your relentless pursuit of excellence are exactly what these fields need.

Opportunities are plentiful. Let us break it down. The opportunities in STEM are vast. Whether you are interested in coding and software development, data analytics, mechanical or electrical engineering, or even biotech and environmental science, there is a niche for you. Do not think for a second that you need a Ph.D. to get started. Sure, advanced degrees can open doors, but there are plenty of entry points that require nothing more than a solid foundation and the willingness to learn. Apprenticeships, certifications, and hands-on experience are just as valuable, if not more so, in many cases. For instance, in the tech industry, the ability to code and understand software architecture can set you up for a career that is both high-paying and in demand. In engineering, the skills to design, test, and improve systems and products are crucial. And with the rise of renewable energy and green technology, there is a growing need for individuals who can innovate in sustainable ways.

The point is, STEM fields are diverse, and the roles within them can cater to a wide range of interests and skills. The Industrial Athlete Advantage Here is why you, as an industrial athlete, are uniquely positioned to thrive in STEM: You already know how to work hard. You are used to putting in the time, pushing through challenges, and staying disciplined. These are the same qualities that will set you apart in STEM fields. While others might struggle with the rigorous demands of these careers, you will already have the mental and physical stamina to keep up and push ahead. Moreover, your practical experience—whether it is in a trade, manufacturing, or any other hands-on field—gives you an edge. STEM is not just about theory; it is about application. You know how to solve problems, you understand the importance of precision, and you are not afraid to get your hands dirty. These skills translate directly to success in STEM. Whether you are troubleshooting a machine, designing a new system, or developing a software solution, your ability to see a project through from start to finish is invaluable. The Payoff Let us talk about the payoff. Careers in STEM are among the highest paying across the board. The median salaries for roles in engineering, technology, and science far exceed those in many other fields. And with the demand for skilled professionals continuing to rise, the job security in these fields is solid. But beyond the financial rewards, there is something even more valuable: the satisfaction of knowing that your work is making a difference. Whether you are developing innovative technologies, improving existing systems, or contributing to scientific research, the impact of your work in STEM can be profound. You are not just punching a clock; you are building the future. That is something worth grinding for. Making the MoveSo how do you get started? First, assess your current skills and see where they align with opportunities in STEM. Are you mechanically inclined? Look into engineering or robotics. Do you have a knack for problem-solving? Data analytics or software development might be your path. Once you have identified your interest, start building your knowledge base. Take courses, get certified, and most importantly, start applying what you learn. The grind does not stop—it just evolves. Remember, breaking into STEM is not about landing a job; it is about positioning yourself in a field that is dynamic, challenging, and rewarding. It is about making the most of your industrial athlete mindset in a space that values innovation and determination. So, do not wait. STEM ahead and start breaking new ground. Your future is waiting, and it is brighter than ever.

The earlier you start, the further you go. That is the mantra when it comes to STEM—Science, Technology, Engineering, and Mathematics—because these fields do not just build careers; they build minds. When you expose kids to STEM from an early age, you are not just setting them up for success in school or work; you are laying the foundation for them to become critical thinkers, problem solvers, and innovators. If you are serious about grinding, if you are serious about building something that lasts, then you already know the importance of getting ahead of the game. But let us dig deeper. Let us talk about the real, measurable benefits of introducing STEM training early on, backed by solid data and research.

Building Cognitive Muscles Early is very critical indeed. Just like you wouldn't expect to bench press 300 pounds on your first day at the gym, you can't expect to solve complex problems without first building the cognitive muscles. Studies show that children who are exposed to STEM concepts at a young age develop stronger critical thinking and problem-solving skills. According to research from the National Science Foundation, early engagement with STEM activities enhances cognitive development, particularly in areas of logic, pattern recognition, and spatial reasoning. These are the building blocks of not just academic success, but of life skills that translate to any field. When kids are introduced to STEM concepts like coding, robotics, or even simple science experiments, they learn to approach problems methodically. They learn that failure isn't the end; it's a step in the process. Just like in martial arts, where each repetition of a move brings you closer to mastery, each attempt at solving a problem in STEM builds resilience and a deeper understanding. They start to see challenges not as roadblocks, but as opportunities to learn and grow. That mindset is priceless. The Confidence Game confidence is a key player in the game of life. You know it, I know it. And guess what? STEM builds confidence in kids. A study from the Girl Scouts Research Institute found that 74% of girls who engage in STEM activities express more confidence in their abilities, compared to only 54% of girls who do not participate in such activities. When kids succeed in solving STEM-related problems, whether it's building a model, coding a simple game, or even just figuring out a math puzzle, it gives them a sense of accomplishment. This success isn't just a pat on the back; it's a psychological boost that tells them they're capable of tackling bigger challenges. Think about it—when you were young, the first time you solved a problem or figured something out on your own, it felt like you could take on the world. That's the feeling we want to foster in kids through STEM. It's not about turning every child into a scientist or engineer; it's about giving them the confidence to pursue their interests, whatever they may be, with the knowledge that they can overcome obstacles. Bridging the Gap in Education and Beyond There's a massive gap in STEM education, particularly when it comes to underrepresented groups—women, minorities, and low-income students. But when you start STEM education early, you begin to bridge that gap. Research from the U.S. Department of Education indicates that students who are engaged in STEM from a young age are more likely to pursue these fields later in life, which can help to level the playing field in terms of career opportunities and earning potential. The economic benefits are clear. According to a report from the Brookings Institution, STEM careers pay significantly more than non-STEM jobs, with the average STEM job paying 26% more than others. And we're not just talking about engineers and scientists; this includes roles in healthcare, information technology, and skilled trades—fields that are accessible to those with the right training. By starting STEM education early, we give kids a fighting chance to access these high-paying, high-growth careers. Futureproofing Careers The world is changing faster than ever, and the jobs of tomorrow are rooted in STEM.

The World Economic Forum (W.E.F) reports that by 2025, many in-demand jobs will require STEM-related skills. Automation, artificial intelligence, renewable energy—these are the industries that will dominate the future. By equipping kids with STEM knowledge early, we're not just preparing them for the jobs of tomorrow; we're giving them the tools to create those jobs. Let's be real success in life is about having options. When you have a solid STEM foundation, your options multiply. You're not boxed into one career path; you can pivot, innovate, and adapt to whatever the future throws at you. That's the kind of leverage you want to build, and it starts with early STEM education. The Grind Starts Early When you introduce kids to STEM, you're teaching them how to grind—how to work through problems, how to push through failures, and how to keep going when things get tough. That's what life is all about. The earlier they learn these lessons, the better equipped they'll be to handle whatever comes their way. So, don't sleep on STEM. Whether you're a parent, a mentor, or someone who just cares about the next generation, make sure they're getting exposed to these fields early on. It's not just about building a career; it's about building a mindset, a set of skills, and a level of confidence that will carry them through life. And if you're serious about the grind, if you're serious about building something that lasts, then you already know the importance of getting ahead of the game. STEM is the future, and the future starts now.

The grind doesn't start when you're 18 and picking a college major or when you're 22 and landing that first job. It starts way earlier, and if you're a parent reading this, know that you've got a front-row seat to one of the most important roles in your child's life—introducing them to the world of STEM. Now, I'm not talking about drilling calculus into your 5-year-old's head. I'm talking about making STEM—Science, Technology, Engineering, and Mathematics—a natural part of their everyday life, so that by the time they're ready to make moves, they've already got the mindset, the skills, and the confidence to go after what they want.

Laying the Foundation

What Parents Can Do So, how do you get started? How do you plant the seeds of STEM early in your child's life? First off, remember that curiosity is the fuel for all STEM learning. Encourage your child to ask questions—lots of them. Don't just give them answers; guide them to find the answers themselves. This builds critical thinking, a core skill in any STEM field. Start with what they love. If your child is into building blocks, you've got an engineer in the making. Introduce them to simple engineering concepts by having them build bridges, towers, or even entire cities. If they're fascinated by the stars, get them a telescope and explore astronomy together. The key is to tie STEM concepts to their interests so that learning feels like play, not a chore. And don't sleep on the power of hands-on experiences. Take them to science museums, tech expos, or even local robotics clubs. These experiences make STEM real to them, not just something they read about in books. If they're old enough, enroll them in coding camps or online courses that teach programming in a fun, interactive way. It's about exposure—letting them see what's possible and giving them the tools to explore it on their own.

Making STEM a Family Affair Let's take it a step further. If you're serious about setting your kids up for success, make STEM a family affair. Work on projects together—build a simple robot, experiment with homemade volcanoes, or even tackle basic coding challenges. This isn't just about teaching them STEM; it's about showing them that learning is a lifelong process, one that you're also committed to. Plus, it strengthens your bond and makes learning a collaborative experience rather than a solo journey. Another key move? Surround them with role models. This could be through books, movies, or even connecting them with professionals in your network who work in STEM fields. Seeing someone who looks like them, talks like them, and comes from a similar background succeeding in STEM can be incredibly powerful. It's about representation and showing them that there's a place for them in these fields.

Global Perspectives

Cultures That Prioritize STEM Now, let's zoom out and look at the bigger picture. Around the world, certain cultures have mastered the art of early STEM education, and we can learn a lot from them. Take Japan, for example. From a young age, Japanese students are immersed in STEM through rigorous math and science curricula. They're taught not just to memorize facts, but to understand underlying concepts and apply them to real-world problems. This focus on deep understanding rather than rote learning is a big part of why Japan consistently ranks high in global STEM achievement. Then there's Germany, where the concept of "dual education" pairs classroom learning with hands-on experience. German students are introduced to technical fields through apprenticeships while they're still in school, giving them a head start in the workforce. This model doesn't just prepare them for jobs; it makes them masters of their craft by the time they graduate. In India, STEM is seen as a pathway to economic stability and upward mobility. Parents and communities place a strong emphasis on math and science from an early age, often supplementing school education with additional coaching and tutoring. This intense focus has helped India produce a significant portion of the world's IT professionals, engineers, and medical experts. China also stands out, especially in how it integrates technology into education from an early age. Chinese students have access to some of the most advanced educational technologies in the world, and the country's focus on producing top-tier engineers and scientists is evident in its rapidly growing tech and innovation sectors. The Chinese education system emphasizes problem-solving, critical thinking, and innovation—skills that are essential in today's STEM-driven world. Bringing It Home So, what can we learn from these global examples? First, that early exposure to STEM matters—big time. Whether it's through school, extracurricular activities, or at home, the sooner you get your kids into STEM, the better. But it's not just about cramming knowledge down their throats; it's about making learning a natural, engaging, and enjoyable part of their lives. Second, the role of parents and communities in supporting STEM education can't be overstated. Whether you're encouraging your child's curiosity, introducing them to new concepts, or simply being there to explore alongside them, your involvement is crucial.

You're not just raising a kid—you're raising a future innovator, problem-solver, and leader. And finally, it's about giving them the tools to succeed in a world that's increasingly driven by science and technology. By fostering an early interest in STEM, you're not just preparing them for a career; you're preparing them for life. You're giving them the skills to adapt, innovate, and thrive in whatever they choose to do. So, let's get to work. Let's start planting those seeds, nurturing that curiosity, and building the next generation of industrial athletes, innovators, and leaders.

Let's talk numbers. Because while passion and curiosity are great motivators, we can't ignore the reality that we all need to eat, pay bills, and hopefully, stack some serious cash along the way. The truth is, if you're looking to build a career or even a future business empire, STEM fields can and will be a part of that. The Earnings Potential in STEM Fields Let's break it down. According to the U.S. Bureau of Labor Statistics, the median annual wage for STEM occupations was significantly higher than the median wage for all occupations. As of the most recent data, STEM workers earned a median salary of about $95,000 per year, compared to around $40,000 for non-STEM workers. That's more than double the earnings, and that's just the median. If you're in a highly specialized field like software development, data science, or certain branches of engineering, those numbers can skyrocket. For example, software developers, who are at the core of our digital world, can expect to pull in an average salary of around $120,000 per year. Data scientists, the people who turn raw data into actionable insights, earn around $110,000 on average. Engineers, depending on their specialization, can see similar numbers. Chemical engineers, for instance, often earn upwards of $108,000, while electrical engineers can make around $103,000 annually. This is just the tip of the iceberg. The tech industry is notorious for offering stock options, bonuses, and other forms of compensation that can push your earnings into the stratosphere. It's not uncommon for top talent in Silicon Valley to have total compensation packages that exceed $200,000 or more when you factor in bonuses and stock. The Entrepreneurial Edge in STEM But it doesn't stop at just getting a high-paying job. The beauty of STEM is that it also offers unparalleled opportunities for entrepreneurship. If you've got a mind for innovation and a knack for solving problems, you can carve out your own path and create something from scratch. Take Elon Musk, for example. He didn't just settle for a comfortable salary; he used his knowledge of physics and engineering to launch companies like Tesla and SpaceX, transforming entire industries in the process. Now, he's one of the richest people on the planet. Let's bring it down to a more attainable level. You don't have to be a billionaire to benefit from the entrepreneurial potential in STEM. Consider the field of biotechnology. With the right idea and some seed funding, you could develop a new medical device, a cutting-edge drug, or even an app that revolutionizes healthcare. The initial costs might be high, but the returns can be astronomical if you're solving a real problem. The biotech industry alone is expected to reach nearly $2.5 trillion by 2025, and there's no reason why you can't grab a piece of that pie. Or think about the opportunities in green technology. With the global push toward sustainability, there's a growing demand for innovations in renewable energy, electric vehicles, and energy-efficient technologies.

Startups in this space are attracting significant investment, and governments worldwide are offering incentives to entrepreneurs who are helping to create a more sustainable future. Then there's the world of cybersecurity. As our lives move increasingly online, the need for security is greater than ever. Cybersecurity startups are booming, and with cybercrime costing the global economy trillions of dollars annually, the potential for growth in this field is enormous. The Global Impact of STEM Entrepreneurship Now, let's take a step back and look at the global picture. Countries that invest heavily in STEM education and innovation are not just producing high-earning individuals; they're driving economic growth on a national level. Take Israel, often referred to as the "Startup Nation." Despite its small size, Israel has one of the highest concentrations of tech startups per capita in the world, thanks to a strong focus on STEM education and military training in tech fields. The result? A thriving economy with a GDP per capita that rivals that of major Western nations. China, too, is a prime example. With massive investments in STEM education and technology, China has rapidly become a global leader in tech innovation.

The country is now home to some of the world's largest tech companies, and its tech sector is a significant driver of its economy. In the U.S., the impact of STEM on the economy is undeniable. The tech industry alone contributes over $1.8 trillion to the U.S. GDP, making up more than 10% of the national economy. And it's not just about big corporations. Small and medium-sized STEM businesses are essential to this growth, driving innovation and creating jobs. The Takeaway Here's the bottom line: STEM is where the money is, both in terms of high-paying jobs and entrepreneurial opportunities. If you're looking to secure your financial future, build generational wealth, or even change the world, STEM gives you the tools to do it. But it's not just about the money. The skills you gain in STEM—critical thinking, problem-solving, innovation—are the same skills that will make you a leader, a creator, and a force to be reckoned with in whatever field you choose. Parents, if you want to set your kids up for success, get them into STEM early. Expose them to the possibilities, support their curiosity, and give them the tools they need to thrive. And if you're already on the path, keep grinding. The rewards are there for those who are willing to put in the work, embrace the challenges, and keep pushing forward. The future is STEM, and it's wide open. The only question is, are you ready to seize it?

PLAYBOOK #8

"MASTERING THE CRAFT: THRIVING IN SKILLED TRADES"

In this world, it is easy to get caught up in the illusion that only white-collar jobs offer the path to success. But let me tell you something real—skilled trades are the backbone of our society. The truth is, mastering a craft in the skilled trades is not just about making a living; it is about thriving in a career where your expertise, dedication, and hands-on experience set you apart from the rest. When you are out there in the field, whether you are welding, laying down brick, or wiring up an electrical system, you are not just working—you are building something tangible, something that will stand the test of time. That is power, my brother. That is legacy. But here is the kicker—thriving in the skilled trades is not just about showing up and doing the job. It is about mastering your craft. It is about being so damn good at what you do that you are irreplaceable. It is about staying hungry, never settling, and always pushing the limits of what you can achieve. This chapter is your blueprint for navigating that path to expertise. We will break down how to master your craft, how to leverage every opportunity, and how to build a career that is bulletproof. Because in the world of skilled trades, it is not just about the work—it is about the grind, the hustle, and the relentless pursuit of excellence.

At the end of the day, even a billionaire must take a dump. And when that golden toilet gets clogged, guess who he is going to call? Someone like me or my guy Al. Al's an airframe and powerplant technician, a person who knows his way around commercial line maintenance, structures, and quality inspection. He is one of the main reasons I took a gamble on myself and decided to level up. I have seen this man go from knocking on doors selling energy plans, to working security in a rent-a-cop uniform at a news station, and then rise to a well-paid aviation professional. Now, here is where it gets interesting. I got hired by a major airline at DTW Metropolitan Airport, but I was just a ramp agent—a fancy way of saying I was the person throwing luggage around. I was grinding out 80 hours a week, not because I wanted to, but because of the way the airline was set up, you could pick up entire shifts if someone else did not want theirs. The catch? It was all straight time, no overtime, no time, and a half. But while I was out there busting my ass, Al had landed a gig at a smaller airline as an aviation tech, and he was lighting a fire under me, pushing me to do better. It was one brutally chilly night, 20 below, and I was on the ramp delivering luggage to a gate. Out of nowhere, I spot Al—or rather, he spots me—and flags me down. Dude's walking down the jet bridge stairs with four cans of soda in his hands. I am like, "Where'd you get those sodas, bro?" He just smirks and nods back at the top of the jet bridge, where a flight attendant is standing, all smiles and waves for Al.

I could not believe it. Here I was, freezing my balls off in a winter poncho and Carhart overalls, and Al's up there getting the VIP treatment for changing a seatbelt and a few light bulbs. So, I walk up to the jet bridge, and as soon as I get up there, the same flight attendant who was all sweet to Al gives me the dirtiest look—like I was the dirt on her shoe. Al comes up behind me, grabs a couple of bags that could not fit in the overhead bins, and slides them down to the ramp. Meanwhile, I am standing there, still in shock at how differently we are being treated. Then, as I am loading the bags, I overhear their conversation. This chick who just gave me the stink eye is now flirting hard with Al, talking about trips and new destinations like they are planning a getaway. But what really got me was when she started trash-talking all the ramp agents—calling us slaves, dirty, useless animals—all while giggling and batting her eyes at Al. After we got back to the TUG carts, Al casually says, "She's only flirting because I'm a mechanic, bro." Then he shows me his paycheck, and I am floored. He is doing double what I am pulling in and doing it in half the hour. That was the moment I knew I had to make a change. Al broke down the entire process for me—aviation school, certifications, the licensing process—and that is when I decided it was time to stop surviving and start thriving. That night was not just cold—it was a wake-up call. It showed me the difference between grinding without a purpose and grinding with a plan. Let me tell you, once you have that plan, the game changes completely. Getting your FAA Airframe and Powerplant (A&P) license is not just about earning a credential; it is about proving to the world that you have the grit, the knowledge, and the hands-on experience to keep aircraft flying safely.

This license is your key to the world of aviation maintenance, and Aerospace, and let me tell you, the process is not for the faint of heart. But if you are serious about leveling up, then this is a path worth grinding through.

Step 1: Get Educated First things first, you must get your foundation right.

That means enrolling in an FAA-approved aviation maintenance technician school (AMTS). This is not some walk in the park—these programs are intense, designed to teach you everything from basic aviation science to advanced aircraft systems. We are talking about

1,900 hours (about 2 and a half months) of training minimum. If you are thinking about skipping this and just learning on the job, let me remind you—this is aviation. There are no shortcuts when lives are on the line.

Step 2: Gain Experience If you did not go the AMTS route, the FAA has another way for you to qualify— by putting in the work.

You need at least 30 months (about 2 and a half years) of hands-on experience working on both airframes and powerplants to qualify. That is real-world, elbow-deep-in-the-engine work. You must show the FAA you can do the job before they think about letting you sit for the exams.

Step 3: Pass the Written Tests...where the rubber meets the road.

There are three written exams you need to pass—General, Airframe, and Powerplant. These tests cover everything you have learned so far, from basic electricity to turbine engine theory. They are tough, but if you have been putting in the work, they are just another step in the process. Each test is 100 questions, and you must score at least 70% to pass.

Step 4: Pass the Oral and Practical Exams Now, this is where it gets real.

The oral and practical exams are conducted by a Designated Mechanic Examiner (DME) who will grill you on your knowledge and skills. You will be tested on your ability to troubleshoot, repair, and inspect various aircraft components. This is not a multiple-choice quiz—this is hands-on, real-world testing. You will have to demonstrate your competence in over 40 subject areas. Fail any section, and you will be going back to the books.

Step 5: Get Your License Once you have passed all the written, oral, and practical exams, the FAA will issue your A&P license.

This is not just a piece of paper; it is proof that you have what it takes to keep aircraft in the air. But remember, the grind does not stop here. This license is just the beginning. You will need to stay current, keep learning, and even add more ratings to your license if you want to keep climbing the ladder. Getting your FAA A&P license is a long, tough road, but it is worth every second. This is not about getting a job—it is about mastering a craft, gaining respect, and proving that you can handle the responsibility of aviation maintenance. This process will test your patience, your knowledge, and your determination, but if you push through, you will come out the other side as a certified aviation maintenance technician—a true master of your craft.

I am happy to admit this was one of the best decisions I have made in my life considering how many doors have opened over my 15+ years in the game. Aviation and Aerospace are obviously the main stars of the show; however, the license allows for a lot more flexibility than most people miss on the first look. This is the part of the game many people overlook but allow me to explain. When people hear about an FAA Airframe & Powerplant (A&P) license, they usually think of one thing—working on aircraft. But let me tell you, this license is like a master key, opening doors to a world of opportunities far beyond just the aviation industry. The real power of an A&P license lies in its versatility. It is not just a piece of paper that says you can work on planes; it is a credential that gives you the skills to troubleshoot, repair, and maintain all sorts of complex systems. If you are smart about it, you can use those skills to carve out a career that suits you, whether that means working for a big-name company, going the entrepreneurial route, or anything in between.

Take troubleshooting, for example. If you have ever been inside a casino, you have seen those rows of slot machines, flashing lights, and digital displays. What you might not know is that many of the skills you learn while earning an A&P license can be applied directly to diagnosing and fixing those machines. That is right—those skills in electrical systems, wiring, and diagnostics are not just limited to aircraft. With an A&P, you can walk into a casino and know exactly what is going on under the hood of those slot machines. Casinos pay good money to keep their machines running smoothly, making this a lucrative side hustle or even a full-time gig if you play your cards right. Now let us talk about the entrepreneurial route. If you have an A&P license, you are sitting on a gold mine of opportunities. For example, you can go independent, set up your own shop as a private mechanic, and cater to a specialized clientele. Pilots, private plane owners, and even small commercial operators all need someone they can trust to keep their aircraft in top shape. Furthermore, you can take it a step further and get your Inspection Authorization (I.A.), you can perform 100-hour or annual inspections, making you even more valuable. This puts you in a position of power, where you are not just another employee but a key player in the aviation ecosystem. Think about the freedom this gives you. With your own business, you control your schedule, your rates, and your clientele. You are not clocking in and out at someone else's convenience—you are building something that is yours.

The demand for skilled A&P mechanics is only growing, meaning you can choose the projects that excite you and leave behind the ones that do not. So, whether you are troubleshooting electrical equipment in a high-stakes casino or inspecting aircraft for high-end clients, the versatility of an A&P license is unmatched. It is a tool that allows you to adapt, evolve, and thrive in a variety of industries. In a world that is constantly changing, having that kind of flexibility is priceless.

PLAYBOOK #9

"NAVIGATING THE FACTORY FLOOR: SUCCESS IN MANUFACTURING"

This is all, one big, beautiful battlefield, little bro. That is what my friend and mentor Mr. G used to tell me when I was grinding it out during my lab sessions on the shop floor in aviation school. He was not just talking about the work; he was talking about life itself—the unseen traps, the invisible landmines ready to blow up your progress if you are not paying attention. "Be mindful, youngster, "he would say. Mr. G was a retiring Army aviation mechanic who had seen it all, working on Apache's and Chinook helicopters, and he knew the game better than anyone. Every time he saw me getting heated over petty favoritism and shop politics, he would tell me to calm down and breathe. See, the politics in school were just a preview of what I would face later in my professional career. My aviation school was split into two schedules: day block and evening block. Different blocks, different instructors, but the same game. If an instructor had a military background, you could bet they would show favoritism to students who had served too. It was like an unspoken rule, a nod to the familiar, and if you were not part of that club, you were on your own. That was my first lesson in shop floor politics, and it was not pretty. I saw professional sabotage, underhanded deals, and what I had later come to call "drug deals"—those backroom agreements where someone is getting hooked up at the expense of someone else. Empathy and familiarity often overshadow logic in these environments, and I learned that the hard way. We have all seen that one guy on the team, the prodigal son, who can do no wrong. No matter what they screw up, they are always given another chance, while you are left to fend for yourself. Harsh lessons like these can do one of two things for you. First, they can help you get out of your own head because idealism only matters if you have the leverage to make it a reality. And second, they teach you the value of being a standout, solo performer. If you cannot win their game, you must create your own lane—build an outstanding record of accomplishment that speaks louder than any favoritism or politics. In the end, it is about survival and success. If you want to rise above the fray, you must play smarter, not just harder. Understand the game, but do not let it consume you. Use the lessons to sharpen your edge, and always stay focused on the bigger picture—your own grind and your own goals.

When you step onto the factory floor of any company, both large and small, you are not just entering a workspace—you are more than likely walking into the heart of an industry that has been the backbone of economies for centuries. Make no mistake, the modern manufacturing sector is different from it was 20 years ago, or even five years ago. It is a battlefield where only the sharpest minds and most skilled hands survive and thrive.

This is not the old-school assembly line where you could coast by doing the bare minimum. No, today's manufacturing is a dynamic, tech-driven environment where precision, efficiency, and innovation are the names of the game. If you are serious about leveling up your career in this space, you have got to understand the rules, the players, and most importantly, how to carve out your own path to success. First things first, know your environment. The factory floor is a complex ecosystem, a well-oiled machine where every part has its role. But do not get it twisted—just because it is a machine does not mean it's mindless. In fact, it's the exact opposite. The manufacturing sector is alive, constantly evolving with innovative technologies like robotics, AI, and advanced materials. If you're not staying ahead of the curve, you're falling behind, Period. To truly navigate this space, you've got to understand its language—cycle times, lean manufacturing, Six Sigma etc. These are not just buzzwords; they are the tools and frameworks that can make or break your career. But more than that, you've got to understand the culture of whatever space you are currently moving through. Manufacturing is about teamwork, precision, and relentless improvement. It is about showing up every day ready to grind, to put in the work, and to push the boundaries of what is possible. Success in manufacturing isn't about knowing how to operate a machine or follow a process. It's about seeing the big picture—how your role fits into the larger goals of the company, and how you can leverage that understanding to advance. It is about recognizing opportunities for improvement, taking initiative, and showing leadership, even if you are not in a formal leadership role. Because on the factory floor, actions speak louder than titles. So, if you are ready to navigate the factory floor like a pro, if you are ready to step up and take control of your career in manufacturing, then buckle up. This journey is not for the faint of heart, but for those who are willing to put in the work, the rewards are limitless. Having a grit about yourself and a long-term outlook will assist you greatly when dealing with the next topic of discussion: "favoritism and or nepotism" top heavy environments.

Workplace favoritism and nepotism are not just annoying—they are toxic, soul-sucking practices that poison the well of productivity and morale. When favoritism and nepotism become the norm, you are not dealing with a healthy work environment; you are navigating a minefield where the rules are rigged, and only the chosen few get a shot at the big leagues. The Toxic Impact of Favoritism and Nepotism can leave unseen lingering damage on a company's legacy as far as overall moral goes. What is the point of training hard, pushing yourself, going beyond if politics and the wave of a pen can derail your ambitions!? Well, that is because it is just your turn, remember? You do not own this company, it is to be treated and viewed as the machine it is, cold, ridged, and dangerous without safety precautions considered on our end. Remember, you are always playing from a defensive posture because you do not possess enough control to sway the company trajectory, you are merely a pawn trying to make it to the other side of the chess board without losing your head, to receive a level-up.

You can play to win or become cannon fodder…the choice is yours. The following are the top 5 things I've personally experience and seen over my 15+ year career you should be aware of when traversing the manufacturing arenas of the world, especially those that favor the "good ole boy system or nepotism"

1. Erosion of Trust

When people see that promotions and benefits are handed out based on personal relationships rather than merit, trust in leadership typically takes a nosedive. A study from the Harvard Business Review shows that favoritism can lead to significant drops in employee engagement and trust. Employees who are not in the inner circle feel demotivated and disconnected because they see their hard work being overshadowed by personal biases. This erosion of trust leads to a toxic atmosphere where people are more focused on who is getting ahead rather than how to succeed themselves.

2. Decreased Morale and Productivity

Favoritism and nepotism do not just mess with the atmosphere—they impact productivity directly. Research published in the Journal of Applied Psychology indicates that employees who perceive favoritism in the workplace are significantly less productive. When people feel their efforts are going unrecognized and that the system is rigged against them, their motivation to go the extra mile evaporates. Instead of striving for excellence, they are just putting in their time, which drags down the whole team's performance.

3. Increased Turnover

Employees who feel they are being overlooked or treated unfairly are more likely to jump ship. The Society for Human Resource Management found that workplaces marred by favoritism and nepotism have higher turnover rates. High turnover is not just a staffing issue—it is a signal of a deeper problem that affects morale, productivity, and the overall health of the organization. Losing experienced employees also means losing institutional knowledge, which can cripple a team's performance and innovation.

4. Stifled Innovation

In environments where favoritism reigns supreme, innovation takes a backseat. When ideas and promotions are based on who you know rather than what you know, it discourages creative thinking and problem-solving. Employees are less likely to propose bold ideas or challenge the status quo if they know their contributions will be overlooked or dismissed. This stagnation can be catastrophic in industries were staying ahead of the curve is critical.

5. Legal and Ethical Issues

Favoritism and nepotism can also expose companies to legal and ethical risks. Discrimination lawsuits and complaints about unfair treatment can damage a company's reputation and lead to costly legal battles. A Forbes article highlights that such practices can result in not only financial repercussions but also long-term damage to a company's brand and employee relations. The Cost of Playing Favorites/Favoritism and nepotism might seem like shortcuts to maintaining power or keeping the peace, but they're just shortcuts to disaster. They erode trust, drag down productivity, increase turnover, stifle innovation, and open a company to legal risks. In a competitive world, where performance and results should be the only currency that matters, playing favorites is a surefire way to undermine everything you've worked for. If you're climbing the ranks or leading a team, remember real success comes from creating a fair, transparent environment where everyone has a shot to shine based on their skills and merits. Only then can you build a thriving, resilient organization where everyone is motivated to grind, excel, and destroy the barriers to success.

The examples provided are in no way a hardline in the sand, but simply a few signpost for anyone reading this to effectively read what the offense is doing or is more than capable of. There's nothing wrong with a father hiring his son on as CEO when if steps down or promoting his favorite nephew to a top managerial role, that's a perk that comes with ownership. I'm simply trying to get you (the reader) to get and or stay out of your feelings when and if you experience this type of environment during your journey.

PLAYBOOK #10

"EFFICIENCY IS KEY: VALUE THE FLOW"

In any field, efficiency isn't just a buzzword; it's the difference between surviving and thriving. When you're grinding in the blue-collar world, where every minute counts and every task has a ripple effect, streamlined workflows become your best ally. Efficiency is the silent power that can elevate your game, helping you accomplish more with less and setting you apart from the pack. It's not just about working harder; it's about working smarter, making every move count like a grandmaster on a chessboard. When you step outside, onto the factory floor, the job site, or even into a meeting room, you're not just there to punch a clock, or take up space—you're there to leave a mark. But how do you do that? How do you stand out in an environment where the tasks are repetitive, and the margins are thin? You master efficiency. You streamline your process to eliminate waste, cut down on unnecessary steps, and focus on what truly moves the needle. To a blue-collar baller, time is currency. Every minute you waste is a dollar left on the table.

The crawl

Let me take you back to a time when I was in the trenches, living paycheck to paycheck, scraping by, and trying to figure out how to make it to the next level. When you are up against the wall, efficiency is not just a luxury—it is a necessity. I was making what I thought at the time to be decent money, but that was a false view, because I did not have a lot of money to show by the end of the month. I had to figure out how to stretch what I had, to maximize every single resource. I was hungry, not just for food, but for a way out, for a better life. I remember getting home after a long day, exhausted and staring at a fridge that was more empty than full. I could not afford the luxury of time, let alone a decent meal, so I started prepping whatever I had. I was not about to waste time thinking about what to eat every day, so I cooked up a big pot of beans and rice, the cheapest and most filling thing I could find. I portioned it out for the week, making sure I had enough to get through. It was not glamorous, but it got the job done. At that point, I focused on mental and physical growth, so gym exercising became a way of life.

I created a home workout routine using nothing but my own body weight and the neighborhood park. No excuses. I saved on transportation by walking or jogging everywhere I could. Any long walks taken, doubled as brainstorming sessions, planning out my next move, figuring out how to get out of the hole I was in. I learned to patch up my own clothes, fixing holes and tears by watching sewing videos via YouTube, instead of buying new ones. Every little bit counted. As for entertainment? Forget about it. I swapped Netflix and nights out for self-education. The local library became my best friend. Free Wi-Fi, free books, and endless knowledge. I spent hours there, reading up on personal finance, business strategies, and anything that could give me an edge.

I wasn't just trying to survive; I was prepping for my future. Slowly but surely, these small, efficient moves added up. I was saving time, saving money, and most importantly, I was creating space in my life to focus on leveling up. Every penny I saved, every minute I squeezed out of the day, went towards my goals. Efficiency wasn't just something I practiced—it was my way out. And when I finally started making moves, that foundation of efficiency became my secret weapon, allowing me to rise when others were stuck in place.

Many will read through this section and say, "that's an extreme way of being", but remember; When you're living under the poverty mindset or just trying to stretch a dollar, efficiency isn't a luxury—it's a necessity. The grind is real, but that doesn't mean you can't make your life more efficient with what you've got.

Methods to maximize your output with limited funds

- **Plan Meals with a Budget:** It is easy to fall into the trap of fast food or junk food because it is quick and cheap. But you can get more bang for your buck by planning meals that stretch across several days. A big pot of chili, a batch of rice and beans, or even pasta can cover multiple meals without breaking the bank.

- **Batch Cooking:** Cooking in bulk not only saves time but money too. Use weekends to prepare meals for the week. Freeze portions, so you always have something ready to go. This saves you from unnecessary takeout or eating out when you're pressed for time.

- **DIY Maintenance:** Whether it is fixing a leaky faucet or patching a hole in the wall, learning basic DIY skills can save you a lot of money. There are countless free tutorials online that can guide you through common household repairs.

- **Public Transportation (Uber/Lyft, etc.):** If owning a car is out of reach, optimize your commute by mastering public transportation. Plan your routes and time carefully, so you are never late. Use travel time to read, listen to audiobooks, or catch up on the news—turning inactive time into productive time.

- **Library Resources:** Your local library is a goldmine of free resources. Beyond books, many offer free access to online courses, audiobooks, and even tools or equipment rentals. Utilize this to build skills and knowledge without spending a dime.

- **Second-Hand Shopping:** Thrift stores, garage sales, and online marketplaces are where you can find everything from clothes to furniture at a fraction of the cost. Quality items often find their way to these spots, so shop smart and do not shy away from used.

- **Use Free Software:** If you need software for work or self-improvement, there are plenty of free alternatives to expensive programs. For example, instead of paying for Microsoft Office, use Google Docs or LibreOffice.

- **Stay Organized:** A cluttered space equals a cluttered mind. Keeping your home, workspace, and schedule organized does not cost much, but it can save you time and mental energy. Make use of what you already have—like repurposing old jars for storage or using boxes to keep things tidy.

- **Barter and Trade:** If money is tight, think about trading skills or goods with friends or neighbors. You can swap babysitting for yard work, or trade baked goods for a haircut. Bartering builds community and gets you what you need without spending cash.

- **Cut Unnecessary Subscriptions:** It is easy to let small monthly subscriptions add up. Whether it is streaming services, apps, or memberships, take a hard look at what you are paying for and cut out what is not essential. Redirect that money into savings or investments that will pay off long-term. This part of the grind is about precision and making smart decisions that maximize every resource you have. When your funds are limited, these strategies can help you stretch further while keeping your goals in sight. Remember, it is not just about surviving—it is about setting yourself up to thrive.

That is why efficiency is king. It is not just about getting the job done; it is about getting it done right, the first time, every time. You eliminate the fluff, cut through the noise, and focus on what really matters. That is how you start to build momentum, how you start to see results not just in your work but in your life. Look at the greats—whether in business, sports, or any other field. They all have one thing in common: they are masters of efficiency. Michael Jordan did not waste time on the court; every move had a purpose. Steve Jobs did not waste time on unnecessary products; he focused on what would change the world (the long game). That is the mindset you need to adopt in your daily grind. But efficiency is not about speed; it is about effectiveness. It is about doing the right things in the right way. This means taking the time to analyze your workflow, identify bottlenecks, and implement changes that streamline your processes. It is about being proactive instead of reactive.

Taking control of your environment, not letting it control you, is the goal. Let us get real—being efficient is not always easy. It takes discipline, focus, and a willingness to change. It means being brutally honest with yourself about where you are wasting time and energy and then having the courage to cut out the dead weight. It is about creating systems that work for you, not against you.

In a world where competition is fierce and resources are limited, efficiency is your secret weapon. It is the edge that will help you outperform, outlast, and outshine. It is the key to unlocking your full potential and achieving the kind of success that does not just pay the bills but builds a legacy. So, do not just work hard—work smart. Look for ways to streamline your workflows, cut out the inefficiencies, and focus on what truly matters. When you do, you will find that you are not just getting by—you are getting ahead.

When you commit to developing efficient life processes, you are not just refining your workflow—you are optimizing your mental game. The psychological benefits of efficiency are deep and transformative. In today's world, where distractions are endless and demands are high, the ability to streamline your life is like gaining a mental superpower. It is about more than just saving time; it is about preserving your mental energy and boosting your overall well-being. According to research published in Psychological Science, when you eliminate unnecessary decisions and tasks from your day, you free up cognitive resources. This is called decision fatigue—each choice you make drains your mental energy. By automating or simplifying repetitive tasks, you preserve your brainpower for the big decisions, the ones that matter most in your career and life. That is why the greats do not sweat the small stuff— they have built systems to handle it as efficiency reduces stress. When you have a clear, streamlined process, you eliminate the chaos and unpredictability that breed anxiety. You know what needs to be done and how to do it, which brings a sense of control and peace of mind.

A study in the Journal of Occupational Health Psychology found that employees who used efficient work practices reported lower levels of stress and higher job satisfaction. The same applies to your personal life—when you have your routines dialed in, you are less likely to feel overwhelmed. Let us talk about confidence. There is a certain swagger that comes from knowing you have your life in order. When you are on top of your game, hitting your goals, and making progress, your self-esteem naturally rises. You start to trust yourself more, which fuels further success. It is a positive feedback loop—the more efficient you become, the more you achieve, and the more confident you grow. This is backed up by research from the American Psychological Association, which shows that mastering tasks and achieving goals boosts self-efficacy, the belief in your own abilities. Finally, efficiency sharpens your focus. When your life is streamlined, you can concentrate on what truly matters without getting sidetracked. This level of focus is essential for deep work, the kind that leads to innovation and breakthroughs.

According to Cal Newport, author of Deep Work, the ability to focus without distraction is becoming increasingly valuable in our information-saturated world. Efficient processes help you cultivate this focus, allowing you to dive deep into your work and produce at a higher level. In short, efficiency is not just a tool—it is a mindset that transforms how you live and work. It gives you more mental clarity, reduces stress, builds confidence, and sharpens your focus. In the grind of life, these psychological benefits give you the edge you need to succeed and thrive. So, if you are serious about leveling up, start by getting your life processes in check.

The payoff is not just in your productivity but in your peace of mind and overall mental strength. Efficiency is not about getting things done faster—it is about building a disciplined process that turns potential obstacles into steppingstones. Throughout history, the people who have mastered this art have not only overcome external opposition but have also defeated their own inner demons. Let us take a closer look at how this has played out, both in the past and in our modern world. Think about Thomas Edison, the man credited with inventing the light bulb. It took him over 1,000 failed attempts to get it right. Most people would have given up after the first few failures, but Edison had a process—an efficient system of experimentation and learning from each mistake. Each failure was just data to him, a step closer to success. His efficiency in managing his experiments allowed him to persist where others would have admitted defeat. Edison did not just overcome the technical challenges—he overcame the internal battle against discouragement and doubt. His process was his weapon, and it made him unstoppable.

Now, let us fast forward to the modern era. Take someone like Tim Cook, the CEO of Apple. When he took over from Steve Jobs, many doubted whether he could maintain Apple's innovative edge. Cook is not a flashy leader; he is known for his operational efficiency and his ability to streamline Apple's processes. Under his leadership, Apple has continued to thrive, becoming the first trillion-dollar company. Cook's emphasis on efficiency—whether in supply chain management or product launches—has allowed Apple to overcome the skepticism and remain at the top of the tech world. His process-driven approach is not about avoiding mistakes; it is about consistently pushing the company forward, even when the market and competition are fierce. Let us bring it down to a personal level. Remember, in your own life, efficiency can be the difference between success and failure, especially when the opposition you face is internal. We all battle with procrastination, self-doubt, and fear of failure. These are the enemies within, and they can be even more dangerous than external obstacles. The key to overcoming them is having a solid process—a routine that you can fall back on, even when your motivation is low. Take the example of James Clear, the author of Atomic Habits. Clear emphasizes the power of small, consistent actions—what he calls "atomic habits"—that, over time, lead to massive results. This approach is rooted in efficiency: breaking down big goals into manageable tasks and creating systems that make those tasks automatic. Clear himself has applied this to his own life, overcoming periods of depression and inertia by focusing on building efficient, repeatable habits. His process became his shield against the internal battles, allowing him to achieve his goals and help millions of others do the same. So, what is the takeaway here?

Efficiency is not just a buzzword—it is a battle strategy. It is about building a process that you can rely on, no matter what opposition you face, whether it is external competition or your own doubts and fears. History and modern success stories show us that those who master this skill are not just surviving—they are thriving, even in the face of overwhelming odds. They are playing the long game, turning every challenge into a chance to refine their process and get one step closer to their goals. If you want to succeed, do not just aim for efficiency—make it your lifeline. Develop a process that keeps you moving forward, no matter what.

At the end of the day, it is not just about working hard; it is about working smartly, consistently, and relentlessly. That is how you grind your way to the top, no matter what stands in your way. I've been fortunate enough to survive within my respective arenas long enough to recover from early beatings, lessons, and resourceful enough thanks to developing a figure-it-out style of accomplishing goals, to not only stack and accumulate money at a higher rate, but I was also able to do so without stretching myself too thin in the process. Fast forward to present day, I am in the top 10% as far as net worth, and I have adopted a leadership mindset that I wield through my life, even when it comes down to so called mundane tasks via outsourcing. I realized that having money is useless to a person without proper time to plot and plan the most optimal way of using his or her money. Like a master sculptor, we too must strip away all inessentials from our day to day living situation. Many want to buy their 24 hours back, and while that sounds cool, I have learned that you must buy it back incrementally in most cases. Take advantage of the current era we live in and be grateful to be born in such a time, as technology has afforded many of us massive opportunity to streamline our lives so we can focus on increasing our strengths and strengthening our weaknesses also. Efficiency helps to free time from the high walls of burdens we construct out of a false sense of fear.

When you are trying to maximize your output, efficiency is not just a concept—it is a lifestyle. It is about making every minute count so you can stay locked in on the grind without unnecessary distractions. The less time spent thinking about the mundane, the more energy you can direct toward your goals. As we level up, so must our overall processes and procedures.

Things you can do to level up efficiency:

- **Hire a Cleaning Service:** A clean environment equals a clear mind. By outsourcing this task, you eliminate the time spent on chores and create space for higher-level thinking and planning. When your home is spotless, your mind can be too.

- **Meal Prep Delivery Services:** Nutrition is key, but meal planning, shopping, and cooking can drain hours from your week. Subscribing to a meal prep service ensures you get healthy, balanced meals without the time commitment. This frees up hours for workouts, reading, or grinding toward your next goal.

- **Automate Your Finances:** Set up automatic bill payments and investments. This removes the risk of missed payments and ensures your money is working for you behind the scenes. The time you save here can be reinvested into learning or executing on your side hustle.

- **Use Smart Home Devices:** Automate lighting, temperature control, and even your morning coffee. These smart devices handle the small stuff, giving you one less thing to think about.

Efficiency means you do not waste brainpower on tasks that technology can handle.

- **Optimize Your Commute**: If you cannot eliminate your commute, make it productive. Listen to audiobooks, podcasts, or even practice a new language. This transforms quiet time into learning opportunities, turning minutes into mental gains.

- **Delegate Tasks:** Whether at work or home, if someone else can do it faster or better, let them. Delegation is not a weakness—it is recognizing where your time is most valuable. Spend your time where it matters most, not on tasks that anyone could do.

- **Batch Tasks**: Group similar tasks together and knock them out in dedicated blocks. This reduces the mental load of switching between tasks and helps maintain focus. For example, handle all your emails or calls in one go instead of letting them interrupt your day.

- **Create Routines:** Establish daily and weekly routines that streamline decision-making. When you know what your day looks like before it even starts, you cut down on decision fatigue and stay on track.

- **Minimize Distractions:** Identify what steals your time and eliminate it. This could be mindless scrolling on social media, unnecessary meetings, or even clutter in your workspace.

- Whatever it is, get rid of it, then **Invest in the Right Tools:** Whether it is a high-powered computer, a planner that works for you, or software that automates repetitive tasks, investing in the right tools can make your workday exponentially more efficient. Efficiency is not about doing everything yourself—it is about leveraging resources and technology to amplify your efforts. The less time you waste, the more you can invest in building the life and legacy you want.

PLAYBOOK #11

"GOALS THAT GROW: THE POWER OF REALISTIC AMBITION"

Ambition can light a fire under you, pushing you to hustle harder, grind longer, and aim higher. But let us be real ambition without clarity is like driving a race car with no steering wheel. You might be going fast, but you are headed straight for a crash. Drive and self-regulation are crucial, but if you are not seeing things clearly, you are setting yourself up for a life of chaos, frustration, and goals that feel more like chains than achievements. Here is the thing—too many of us get caught up in comparing our grind to the next person's, thinking that if we just do what they are doing, we will get what they have gotten. That is a recipe for disaster. You must understand that clarity is the secret sauce to making your ambitions work. It is not just about wanting more; it is about knowing exactly what you want, why you want it, and how to go after it without losing yourself in the process. Look, we have all been there choosing a career or a path because it looked like the perfect adventure from the outside, only to find out it is not what we expected. That is what happens when your eyes get bigger than your stomach. Just like you cannot eat a feast in one sitting without paying the price, you cannot achieve massive goals without building up your capacity over time. Your brain, like your stomach, needs to stretch and expand gradually. You do this by feeding it a steady diet of experiences, experiments, failures, losses, and wins. Each one of those things is a rep in the gym, a step on the ladder, a brick in the foundation. I used to think just having a job was the endgame. I thought if I could just get my foot in the door, I would be set.

Let me tell you, that mindset was a bubble—a bubble of confinement that kept me from seeing the bigger picture. Sure, it was better than not having money, but it was not enough. It was not until I started to feel that bubble tightening around me again that I realized I needed more. I needed to expand, to push past the boundaries I had set for myself. That is when the lessons started hitting hard. I had to learn that hindsight is not just for looking back and wishing things were different; it is for reflecting, learning, and making sure you do not make the same mistake twice. If you are not clear about where you are going, you are just wasting time. Ambition without clarity is like setting sail without a compass. You will move, but you will never reach your destination. So, before you let your drive take you to the next level, make sure you are seeing things for what they are. Be honest with yourself about what you really want, and do not be afraid to adjust your course. Because the only thing worse than not reaching your goals is reaching the wrong ones and realizing you have wasted your time chasing someone else's dream. You would think during a time when information is readily available on lighting tap that millions of humans would take full advantage, resulting in mass innovation, newly discovered scientific breakthroughs, cures for diseases, inventions etc. Instead, we have heard mentality in-mass across the board. (at least in the western world) that does nothing but stifle growth, and bold action.

The Brick-by-Brick Brain strategy

Simply put, both the human brain and subconscious keep score as it relates to our growth mindset and or regressive behaviors and thoughts. Let us get one thing straight—your brain is like a muscle. It needs consistent training and the right kind of fuel to grow stronger. Just like you would not expect to bench press 300 pounds if you have never lifted more than 150, you cannot expect your mind to fully believe in a $10,000-a-month goal if the most you have ever brought in is $4,000. Your brain needs evidence. It needs proof that you can win, that you are capable, that your ambitions are not just fantasies—they are achievable milestones. When you set a goal that's way beyond anything you have achieved before, your brain will fight you on it. It is wired to protect you, to keep you in your comfort zone. So, if you are aiming for $10,000 a month but have only ever seen $4,000, your mind is going to throw up all sorts of doubts, fears, and reasons why it is not possible. You need to feed your brain a steady stream of wins to build up its confidence, to show it that this new goal is not just a pipe dream. It is the next logical step. Research shows that the human brain is a pattern-seeking machine. It thrives on repetition and incremental growth. When you set and achieve smaller, realistic goals, you are creating a record of accomplishment of success. Each win, no matter how small, is like a deposit into your mental bank. Over time, these deposits add up, giving you the confidence and the evidence you need to go after bigger goals. This is what psychologists refer to as self-efficacy—the belief in your ability to succeed in specific situations. The more you succeed, the more your brain believes that you can succeed again.

A study published in Psychological Review highlights the importance of gradual progress and the power of self-efficacy. The research shows that when people set goals slightly above their current capabilities and then achieve them, they experience a boost in confidence and motivation. This incremental approach to goal setting helps create a solid foundation upon which larger ambitions can be built. It is like laying bricks—each one supports the next, and before you know it, you have constructed something massive, something that once seemed impossible. So, if you are serious about leveling up your income from $4,000 to $10,000 a month, start by breaking it down. What is the next achievable step? It is $5,000, then $6,500. Each time you hit a new target, your brain registers that as proof of your capability. With each win, your belief in the possibility of $10,000 grows stronger, and your mental resistance diminishes. You are not just thinking about $10,000 anymore—you are actively creating the conditions necessary to achieve it. Understand that t is not just about the money, or money at all. This principle applies to every area of your life.

Whether it is fitness, relationships, or personal development, your brain needs a record of accomplishment of success to support improved goals. Do not just tell yourself you are going to do it—show yourself you can do it. Stack those wins, build that evidence, and watch how your mind starts to expand its own possibilities. In the end, realistic ambition is not about playing small. It is about respecting the process, understanding that growth is a step-by-step journey. You must put in the work, build the foundation, and let your ambition stretch as your mind grows stronger. Because when you have a solid record of accomplishment, when you have proven to yourself that you can achieve the small goals, the big ones stop looking so impossible. They start looking like the next step in your journey—just another grind that you are more than capable of mastering.

The counterintuitive approach

Growth is not about the glamorous, Instagram-worthy highlights. It is about the grind, the setbacks, the discomfort that no one wants to talk about, but everyone who has ever made real progress knows all too well. You want those shredded biceps, the kind that make heads turn? Then you must be prepared to tear those muscles apart first. Day in and day out, you will hit the gym, pushing yourself past what is comfortable, breaking down muscle fibers just to build them back up again. But here is the kicker—if you are doing it right, it is going to hurt. A lot.

Now, let us flip the script for a second. What if you were told upfront that chasing your goals would mean waking up every day with your body screaming in pain, feeling like you have been hit by a truck? That the road to those giant biceps is paved with soreness so intense, you can barely lift your arms to brush your teeth? How many people do you think would still sign up for that? Few, I had bet. See, that is where the counterintuitive part comes in. We have all heard it— "No pain, no gain." It is a simple mantra, easy to repeat, but it holds a deeper truth that is not always obvious. The pain is not just a side effect; it is the process. The very discomfort you are trying to avoid is what is going to forge the new you. Most people do not want to hear that, instead, they want the results without the grind, the gains without the struggle. Think about it this way: Imagine you are a boxer preparing for a fight. You do not get better by just practicing your punches. You get better by taking hits, by putting yourself in the ring against opponents who push you to your limits. Every punch you take conditions your body, sharpens your reflexes, and hones your mind. But if you fear getting hit, if you shy away from the pain, you will never reach your full potential. Pain is not just an obstacle—it is a part of the path. Or take another example—someone grinding to make a name in their career.

They want to level up, to reach that six-figure salary, but all they see are the late nights, the missed weekends, the constant grind that is sucking the life out of them. It is easy to get discouraged, to want to tap out when the pressure starts to feel unbearable. But here is the reality—those sleepless nights, those high-stress moments? This is not just part of the journey; it is the journey. That is the crucible that refines your skills, your resilience, your ability to handle the next level.

There is a reason so many people fail to reach their goals—they are not willing to embrace the pain. They've sold this idea that success should be easy, that if you struggling, you must be doing something wrong. But the truth is, struggle is where the magic happens. The pain is where you grow. The people who truly succeed are the ones who learn to lean into it, who understand that discomfort is not something to be avoided, but something to be embraced. Now, let us bring it back to that "No pain, no gain" mantra. It's not just about fitness—it's a mindset, a way of life. Whether you're in the gym, in the office, or out in the world chasing your dreams, remember that pain is a sign you are on the right path. It is proof that you are pushing your limits, that you are growing. So instead of running from it, run towards it. Embrace the discomfort, because on the other side of that pain is the person you are working to become.

The Martial arts Mindset for Growth

When we talk about pain and growth, it's not just about hitting the gym or working late nights at work. This concept has been around for centuries, and no group understood it better than the samurai. These warriors lived by a strict code that wasn't just about mastering the sword, but about mastering themselves—mind, body, and spirit. They knew that to reach the peak of their abilities, they had to embrace discomfort, pain, and the daily grind. Take the samurai training process as an example. A young samurai didn't become a master swordsman overnight. His journey began with rigorous, repetitive drills—thousands of hours spent perfecting the same strike, repeatedly. These exercises weren't glamorous; they were grueling. The purpose wasn't just to hone technique, but to forge mental toughness. Each swing of the sword was an exercise in discipline, in pushing past the limits of the body to strengthen the mind. The pain from endless training sessions wasn't something to be avoided; it was the very thing that sharpened their skills, making them deadly in battle. This concept is echoed in martial arts philosophy, particularly in the teachings of Miyamoto Musashi, one of the most famous samurai and strategists of all time. Musashi wrote about the idea of "embracing the way of the warrior," which meant understanding that pain, hardship, and struggle were essential to becoming a true master. Musashi wasn't just talking about physical pain—he was talking about the mental struggle of constantly pushing yourself beyond what you thought was possible. The discipline to keep going, even when everything in you wants to quit, is what separates the master's from the average. Now, let's bring it to modern times with another martial arts legend, Bruce Lee. Lee wasn't just a martial artist; he was a philosopher who understood the importance of embracing pain as part of the growth process. He once said, "Do not pray for an easy life, pray for the strength to endure a difficult one." This quote embodies the counterintuitive approach. Lee knew that the pain and struggle he faced in his training were the keys to unlocking his true potential. He pushed his body to the breaking point because he understood that the real battle was with himself—his doubts, his fears, his limitations. The wisdom of the samurai and martial arts masters like Bruce Lee teaches us that the path to greatness isn't easy, and it isn't supposed to be. It is about embracing the grind, loving the process, understanding that the pain is necessary to achieve new levels of strength, and realizing that each struggle is a step toward mastery.

Whether you are swinging a sword or lifting weights, practicing a skilled trade, developing a new skillset etc.... the principle is the same— the discomfort you feel is the fire that forges your strength. So, when you are facing challenges in your own life, whether it is in the gym, at work, or in your personal growth, remember the lessons of the samurai. Embrace the pain. Lean into the discomfort. Understand that each struggle is an opportunity to sharpen your skills, to strengthen your mind, and to prepare yourself for whatever battles lie ahead. That is the path to mastery, and it is a path that has been walked by a few for centuries. Now, it is your turn.

PLAYBOOK #12

"THE WARRIOR'S EDGE: CULTIVATING A SELF-IMPROVEMENT"

I am not cocky at all...I am simply better than them, and that older version of myself, my friend Khalil would say especially when confronted by anyone with a negative disposition or limiting beliefs. Khalil was what I would like to call a work-in-progress practitioner. Never mastering one specific thing, but fully embracing the overall process as his mission. In his view; why stressing over one specific skill that could fail you or become obsolete when you could become a master at the "permanent pivot technique"

In the battlefield of life, the mind is your most powerful weapon. But like any weapon, it requires regular sharpening, maintenance, and a relentless commitment to improvement. That is the edge, the advantage that separates those who merely survive from those who thrive. This is the mindset of a warrior, someone who does not just adapt to change but actively seeks it out, refines themselves, and uses every experience as fuel for growth. This is not just motivational talk—there's solid science behind why committing to continuous personal and professional growth is crucial for your brain and overall well-being. The Science of Continuous Improvement The brain is a remarkably adaptable organ, a concept known as neuroplasticity. This means that your brain can change, adapt, and grow in response to new experiences and learning. According to research published in Nature Reviews Neuroscience, when you challenge yourself with new skills, ideas, or environments, your brain forms new neural connections, rewiring itself. This process not only enhances cognitive functions but also improves your ability to handle stress, solve problems, and innovate. Think about that for a second: by committing to continuous improvement, you are upgrading your mental hardware. You are not just learning; you are increasing your brain's capacity to learn. This is why people who embrace lifelong learning often find themselves getting sharper, more creative, and more resilient as they age, while those who remain stagnant tend to experience cognitive decline. Moreover, studies from the Journal of Clinical Psychology have shown that individuals who set and pursue personal and professional growth goals report higher levels of life satisfaction and psychological well-being.

The act of striving towards something meaningful gives your life direction and purpose, which are critical components of mental health. The Benefits of Well-Being Let us talk about well-being for a moment. Continuous improvement does not just make you smarter—it makes you happier and healthier too. When you engage in activities that challenge you and lead to personal growth, your brain releases dopamine, the "feel-good" neurotransmitter. This dopamine rush is what makes achieving goals so satisfying and why setting and meeting new challenges can be downright addictive. Never been about feeling good in the moment, it is a gradual build-up over time.

The process of setting and achieving goals also builds self-efficacy, or your belief in your ability to succeed. According to research published in the Annual Review of Psychology, higher self-efficacy is associated with lower levels of stress, better emotional regulation, and an increased ability to bounce back from setbacks—traits that are essential for both personal and professional success. Furthermore, a study from the Journal of Happiness Studies found that people who continuously strive for improvement tend to have lower levels of anxiety and depression. This is because the act of setting goals and working towards them provides a sense of control over your life, counteracting the feelings of helplessness that often lead to mental health issues.

The Warrior's Approach So, how do you cultivate this warrior's mindset of continuous improvement? It starts with understanding that growth is not a one-time event; it is a lifelong journey. You must be relentless in your pursuit of bettering yourself, whether through learning new skills, expanding your knowledge, or pushing your physical and mental limits.

Few strategies to get you started

SMART Goals:

These are "**Specific, Measurable, Achievable, Relevant, and Time-bound**" goals. SMART goals give you clarity and a roadmap to success, ensuring that your efforts are focused and productive.

Embrace Failure:

Understand that failure is not the opposite of success; it is a part of the process. Each failure is a lesson, an opportunity to refine your approach and get one step closer to your goal.

Build Resilience:

Practice resilience by pushing through challenges and setbacks. This builds mental toughness, which is essential for continuous improvement.

Seek Feedback:

Do not shy away from constructive criticism. Use it as a tool for growth, a way to identify your blind spots and improve.

Stay Curious:

Never stop learning. Read widely, ask questions, and seek out new experiences, live life with intention. The more you learn, the more you grow. The more you grow, the higher you can reach and touch new levels.

Reflect Regularly:

Take time to reflect on your progress. This allows you to celebrate your successes, learn from your failures, and adjust your goals as needed.

Growth-Minded Inner-circle:

Your environment plays a huge role in your growth. Surround yourself with people who challenge you, support your goals, and inspire you to keep pushing forward.

The Bottom Line Cultivating a self-improvement mindset is not becoming better at what you do; it is about becoming better at being you. It is about unlocking your full potential and living a life that is rich in experiences, knowledge, and satisfaction. The benefits of this mindset extend far beyond your career—they impact your mental and physical health, your relationships, and your overall sense of fulfillment. So, adopt the warrior's edge. Commit to continuous growth, sharpen your mind, and keep pushing your boundaries. The path to mastery is a long one, but every step forward brings you closer to the best version of yourself. And that, my friend, is the true essence of the grind.

PLAYBOOK #13

"THE POWER OF PRESENCE: MANAGING YOUR ENVIRONMENT FOR SUCCESS"

You have probably heard the phrase "Be where your feet are," and it might have gone in one ear and out the other like one of those motivational sayings on a coffee mug. But let me tell you right now—presence, real, focused presence—is a notable change. In a world obsessed with distractions, mastering the ability to be fully present in the moment is a weapon. It is a skill that can help you dominate your space, improve your productivity, and most importantly, keep your mental health on point. Presence is not about mindfulness or some philosophical idea—it is backed by solid science, and when you understand how to manage it, you can transform not only your environment but your entire life.

The Science of Being Present

Psychologically speaking, being present—also called mindfulness—isn't just about feeling good or staying calm. It's about optimizing your brain to function at its highest potential. Research from Harvard University showed that people spend about 47% of their waking hours thinking about something other than what they're currently doing. That's almost half your day spent not focused on the task in front of you. Think about that wasted potential. This lack of focus leads to inefficiency, more stress, and lower overall well-being. It's like trying to run a race with one foot in the air. You won't get anywhere fast. But when you're fully present, your brain works at a higher capacity. According to The American Psychological Association, people who practice being mindful are more likely to perform well under pressure, manage stress more effectively, and experience higher levels of satisfaction with their work and personal lives. It's all about harnessing the power of now. When you're fully in the moment, your brain shifts into what's known as a flow state, where time seems to stand still, and your laser-focused on the task at hand. Athletes know this as "being in the zone," and it's not just for the elite few—it's a state anyone can reach by mastering presence.

Environment and Presence: Setting Yourself Up for Success

Now, you might be thinking, "How do I stay present when everything around me is chaos?" And that's a valid question. Your environment plays a huge role in how easily you can tap into that presence. If your space is cluttered, filled with distractions, or doesn't inspire you, it's going to be damn near impossible to stay focused.

Let's break down how to manage your environment to support that state of presence:

1. Declutter Your Physical Space

   A cluttered space leads to a cluttered mind. Princeton University Neuroscience Institute conducted a study showing that physical clutter negatively impacts your ability to focus and process information. Clean up your workspace, get rid of unnecessary distractions, and create an environment that promotes focus. Less visual noise means more mental clarity.

2. Control Your Digital Environment

Technology is a double-edged sword. While it can be a powerful tool for productivity, it's also one of the biggest distractions. Studies have shown that it takes an average of 23 minutes to refocus after a distraction. That's almost half an hour of lost productivity every time your phone buzzes. Set boundaries—turn off notifications, block out dedicated work times, and create digital habits that help you stay present.

Use Your Environment as a Trigger for Presence

Make your space work for you. If you associate certain places or activities with presence and focus, you're more likely to tap into that mindset when you enter those spaces. For example, a quiet corner of your home could become your go-to spot for deep work or reflection, and over time, just sitting there will trigger your brain to switch into focus mode.

Historical and Modern Examples of the Power of Presence

History is littered with examples of people who harnessed the power of presence to their advantage. Let us start with the samurai of feudal Japan. These warriors were not just physically strong—they were mentally disciplined, practicing zanshin, a state of relaxed alertness and presence. The samurai understood that being fully present in the moment, whether in combat or daily life, was critical to their survival and success. They trained their minds to focus entirely on the task at hand, whether it was a duel or sharpening their blade. This intense level of focus and presence was often the difference between life and death. Now, fast-forward to the modern era. Steve Jobs, the co-founder of Apple, was known for practicing mindfulness and meditation. In fact, Jobs credited much of his creativity and success to his ability to stay present. In his own words, he said, "If you just sit and observe, you will see how restless your mind is... If you try to calm it, it only makes it worse, but over time it does calm, and when it does, there's room to hear more subtle things—that is when your intuition starts to blossom."

His ability to stay present allowed him to think creatively and make decisions that revolutionized the tech industry. Another example is LeBron James, one of the greatest basketball players of all time. LeBron is known for his ability to perform under immense pressure, often during the most critical moments of a game. He attributes much of his success to his mental preparation and his practice of mindfulness, which helps him stay present and focused, even when the stakes are at their highest.

Why Presence Matters for You

Here's the bottom line: presence is the ultimate productivity hack. It's the foundation of self-discipline, the fuel for creativity, and the key to unlocking your highest potential. Whether you're building your empire, grinding through a 9-to-5, or chasing personal goals, learning to manage your environment and control your focus will give you an edge. Start by evaluating your current situation. Are you constantly distracted? Is your space working against you instead of for you? Make the necessary adjustments and watch how much easier it becomes to get in the zone and crush your goals. Remember, presence isn't just about working harder—it's about working smarter. It's about maximizing every moment and putting yourself in the best possible position to win. In the words of one of my mentors, "Be where your feet are, and you'll go further than you ever imagined.

The Takeaway:

Master your environment, manage your presence, and success will follow. Because in the end, it's not just about what you do—it's about how present you are when you do it.

"THE LOCKER ROOM: POST GAME RECAP"

The recap is always a crucial step in the process. It is that moment you allow yourself to leapfrog back in time, tapping into hindsight like a tool that sharpens your edge for the next round. But here is what you must remember—no matter what has happened, no matter who doubted you, no matter the odds, at the end of the day, it is you vs. you. That is, it. No one else is driving this ship. Those quiet nights alone when the noise fades, and it is just you and your thoughts—that is when the real talk begins. That is when you face yourself. It is in these moments, after all the hype dies down, after the lights turn off, that you wrestle with your decisions: the moves you made, the ones you did not make, and the ripple effects of both. You will ask yourself the tough questions: Did I leave it all on the field? Could I have done more? Should I have taken that risk? Those self-reflections will haunt you if you let them, but they will also be your greatest teacher if you pay attention. I will be real with you—authoring this book was not just about offering you some blueprint. It was about holding up a mirror. And as I sat down to write, I often found myself torn because deep down, I know something that most people will not admit I cannot save everyone. As much as I want to help, as much as I want to see you win, not everyone will get this message. Not everyone will be able to stomach the raw truth it takes to get to the top. You know what? That is okay.

The Few That Will Get It

It is a hard pill to swallow, but here is the reality: only a select few are going to get this far. Only a few will read these words and really feel them in their bones. Most will skim, nod, and move on to the next thing, caught up in the illusion of busyness. But there is a reason, in every aspect of life, there is only a top 1%, or even a top 10%—because the majority are not willing to grind, to sacrifice, to go beyond what is comfortable. That is not a negative outlook. It is just facts. And the sooner you embrace that, the quicker you will move toward your own personal greatness. The masses are always going to chase distractions, but the real ones, the ones who are truly about that life, are focused on one thing: building themselves into something unbreakable. So, if you are still with me at this point, you are one of the few. You see beyond the surface. You understand the method to the madness, the rhythm beneath the chaos. You get that the grind is not about fast results, but long-term impact. You know that every setback, every failure, every sleepless night is part of the blueprint. You do not just see the plan— you respect it. You welcome it, and remember you Are Your Own Competition.

Look, you have heard it a thousand times: it's you vs. you. But I do not think most people really understand what that means. This isn't some motivational poster. This is life. Every decision you make, every excuse you let slip through, every moment you choose to be lazy instead of disciplined—that is a battle with yourself. That is, you choosing to either build or destroy. It is easy to get caught up in external competition. You see other people winning, or you see someone getting ahead of you, and it messes with your head. But let me tell you something—the only opponent that truly matters is the man in the mirror. Everyone else is just a distraction. They are background noise. The real fight is internal. It is about whether you have the discipline to keep showing up, to keep pushing yourself when no one is watching, when no one is cheering you on. The biggest obstacle you will ever face is your own comfort zone. That is the real opponent. Comfort will seduce you into thinking you have done enough, that you deserve to coast, that you do not have to keep grinding because you have already made it past some imaginary finish line. But success does not have a finish line. There is no endgame to growth. The moment you think you've "made it" is the moment you start losing.

The Mental Fight

So, here is the real deal: this journey is not about being the best at everything. It is about being the best version of yourself. That is the fight, and you are going to take punches. Life is going to throw some haymakers at you. You are going to fail. You are going to question your path. And in those dark moments, it is easy to start pointing fingers, to blame circumstances, other people, bad luck, whatever. If you are really in it for the long haul, if you are really committed to leveling up, you will stop looking for external reasons and start holding yourself accountable. There's power in owning your setbacks. There's power in saying, "Yeah, that was on me. I dropped the ball." Why? Because it puts the control back in your hands. It means you have the power to fix it. It means you can change the outcome next time. But if you keep blaming everyone and everything else, you are handing your power over to something or someone outside of you. If you are not in control, you cannot win. That is the essence of the post-game locker room talk. It is where you strip away all the BS, look yourself in the eye, and decide: Am I going to do better? Am I going to be better? And if the answer is yes, then get ready to lace up and go another round.

Legacy Over likes

Let us talk about legacy. Because when all is said and done, when the grind is over, and the lights go out, that is what is left. Your legacy. Not the likes you got on social media, not the approval from people who do not even matter. But the impact you made, the lives you changed, the work you put in that cannot be erased. That is what matters. That is what you are building toward every single day. Legacy is not built by chasing trends or cutting corners. It's built by doing the hard work, by staying consistent, by making the tough choices that most people avoid. It's about delayed gratification, knowing that the sacrifices you make today will pay off tenfold down the road.

When you're sitting in that post-game locker room, reflecting on your journey, ask yourself: What am I leaving behind? What mark am I making on the world? Because at the end of the day, it's not about being remembered by everyone—it's about being remembered by the right people, the ones who matter, the ones who were impacted by the life you lived. The question now is, what are you going to do next? Are you going to be a spectator in your own life, or are you going to be the one running the plays? It's easy to watch from the sidelines, but legacy is built by those who are in the game, putting in the work, play after play, no matter the score. That Airframe & Powerplant License you've been thinking about? That's a key, but it isn't the destination—it's just a tool. Your STEM education? A blueprint, but it's not the whole building. Presence and mindset? That's your internal fuel, but you have got to fill the tank every damn day. The point is, all these pieces work together to help you build—but the work? That's on you. No one's going to hand you anything, no one is going to walk your path for you. You must want it enough to go after it, even when it feels like the odds are stacked against you. Make no mistake, the odds will be stacked against you. Life does not care about your plans or your dreams. It's indifferent. But that's where the power of presence comes in. When you can focus on what's right in front of you, when you can dominate your space, your time, and your effort, the world bends to your will. The impossible becomes achievable. That is the difference between people who talk about success and people who live it.

Here is something that has stuck with me through the years: You are the architect of your own life. And architects do not just look at a blueprint once and stop for the day. They refine it, adjust it, troubleshoot it, until the vision comes to life. Your goals, your ambitions? That is your blueprint. But the process? The day-to-day grind? That is where the real work happens. Look, it is easy to set big goals. You can say you want to make $10,000 a month, but if you are only making $4,000 right now, you have some work to do. You must build a foundation strong enough to hold that weight. And that foundation is built with small wins. Incremental progress. You do not just leap from $4K to $10K overnight. You must stack those victories, build that confidence, prove to yourself, brick by brick, that you are capable of more. And each time you win, your mind expands, your vision gets clearer, and your ambition gets sharper. That is why you cannot skip the struggle. The grind is where the magic happens. It is where you cultivate resilience, discipline, and the kind of focus that cannot be shaken. And when you are in that post-game locker room, reflecting on your journey, it is those moments of struggle and perseverance that will mean the most. Because they are proof that you did not quit when it got hard. So, as we wrap this up, I am going to leave you with a choice. You have two paths in front of you. You can either go back to what is comfortable, to what you have always done, or you can push yourself to build something new. Destroy the outdated version of you that played it safe, that doubted your abilities, that let fear dictate your moves. And build the version of you thatis nott afraid to take risks, to face failure head-on, to keep grinding even when no one else is watching. Success does not happen in a vacuum. It happens in the grind, in the day-to-day struggle, in the late nights and early mornings.

In quiet moments, like this one, when you are left with nothing but your own thoughts. That is when you decide who you really are. So here we are. You have made it to the end of the book. But if you think this is the end of your journey, you have it twisted. This is just the beginning. Everything we have talked about—the grind, the setbacks, the discipline, the mindset—it is all prep work. The challenge starts when you close this book and step back into the world. This is your life. This is your fight. It is not going to be easy. But you already knew that. So now, it is time to make a choice: Are you going to build, or are you going to destroy? You already know the answer to that question by now. You ever sit down after a long day, body sore, mind exhausted, and just breathe? That deep breath where your chest finally relaxes, and for a split second, the world feels quiet. That is the moment—the post-game locker room talk. Whether you won or lost, you are sitting there, processing, reflecting on the grind, the sweat, the wins, and the L's. This does not mean the end, it is just the intermission before the next round, the next fight, the next opportunity. In this space, this is where you decide: do I keep building, or do I destroy? That is what this whole journey was about. It is not just the blood, sweat, and tears you put into your chosen path. It is not just the goals you chase or the obstacles you face. It is about understanding that every day is a choice—to build yourself up or tear yourself down. Please do not ever get it twisted, sometimes destruction is necessary.

You must break down old habits, outdated mindsets, toxic people, and environments that keep you stagnant. But after that demolition comes the real work: the building phase. We started this conversation talking about goals, ambition, all the way down to the power of presence. Now we are here in the locker room, chopping this fable of yours…looking back at everything we have covered. I hope you feel different now—I hope you feel ready, because if you do not, it is time to check your pulse. Here is the truth no one wants to tell you: the grind is ugly (Always). It is not always Instagram-worthy or filled with highlight reels. The grind will break you down, humble you, make you question yourself in ways you never thought possible. But the grind is also where you find out who you really are. You know what separates the pros from the amateurs? Resilience. When the pressure is on, when the walls start closing in, do you fold, or do you fight? When you get knocked down, do you get back up, or do you stay on the mat? That is the post-game locker room talk right there—it is that honest conversation you have with yourself about whether you are really cut out for this. If you are sitting there wondering, doubting if you have what it takes, let me remind you: You have made it this far. You have survived every difficult day, every setback, every "no," every closed door. You are still standing, and that means more than you know, so keep learning what that means.